ALL THIS
And A Book

ISBN 978-1-907881-78-7 (Hardback)
ISBN 978-1-907881-79-4 (Paperback)
10 9 8 7 6 5 4 3 2 1

First published in 2018 by Hadean Press
West Yorkshire
England

WWW.HADEANPRESS.COM

ALL THIS
And A Book

Cath Thompson

For Jim

James Lees, 2008.

TABLE OF CONTENTS

"Be a good witness."

Jake Stratton-Kent

Intro...

THE TITLE OF this book comes from *Liber AL* III: 39, "All this and a book to say how thou didst come hither...". It's a quote I earmarked years ago as being suitable for a history of the English Qaballa. In 2013 I completed the first version which was built upon a structure I had planned in the 1980's, and comprised a series of essays and short articles. It was a dry and factual account of the discovery and development of the Qaballa; Jim read it and pencilled a note in the margin to the effect that it was in need of anecdotes. I thought the title good, and in 2016 I wrote a second draft telling of my thirty-odd years involvement with the O∴A∴A∴ and the initiatory experiences which come with E. Qaballistic working. Reading through both texts revealed similarities, repetitions, and omissions, and it seemed best therefore to marry them together; this is the result.

The details in this book are included at my discretion. I do not think I have said too much: if any reader thinks that I have said too little I apologise, and encourage them to redress the balance, if they can.

I must thank all members, past and present, of the O∴A∴A∴, the Continuum, and the O∴A∴A∴ Second Order, for their contributions, too many and various to mention individually, to the development of the English Qaballa in theory and in practice.

Thank you to Erzebet for her boundless enthusiasm and inexhaustible patience.

Thank you to Richard and Will for their hospitality.

Preliminary Elementary Initiation

I WAS SITTING AT a crossroads in the chilly dusk of a still November evening. The year was 1980, and I was just eighteen; I was sitting on the ground at the edge of a path with a big old silver birch tree leaning overhead and the surrounding woodland all rustling and hushing into quiet as the night crept in. I could see the pale gleam of the sandy tracks as they came up out of the young birches in front of me, merging to my right in an irregular lozenge under the open sky, and dividing again to the left and right and away into the wood behind. The paths were bordered with a narrow strip of short grass rising to low dark hedges of drooping bracken. I had walked here along one of them, and my guide had pointed to the birch tree standing like a sentinel of the crossroads, and tinted pink on its higher branches in the afterglow of the sunset.

"Wait there," he said, "someone will come and get you." That was maybe half an hour ago. I had gathered stones and made a modest fireplace a few feet in front of the birch tree, and going into the wood a little way I soon gathered firewood and kindling. The dusk was taking the colour out of the trees on the far side of the path as I got my fire going and settled myself down to wait for my Summoner to bring me to the Initiation known as the Man Of Earth.

There was nothing else to do but wait. I had a photocopy of the candidate's script with me, but it was too dark to read now, the November night had gently enveloped the trees around me, and anyway I was as sure as I could be of my lines and cues. It was just questions, to which I would give answers. I prodded my fire and hugged my knees and went over my responses one more time.

"How do you travel? Answer, In perfect love and perfect trust." That was true enough, otherwise I would not be sitting under a tree in the dark a few months after my eighteenth birthday. I would not have spent two or three days last week making a white robe for this very occasion. And I would not have emptied my pockets in front of my guide so that it was clear that I had nothing but my robe, washed and pressed and folded neatly in a carrier bag, to distract me from the matter in hand.

"Answer, I travel in search of light."

Oh, I wanted that light, as I had never wanted anything before. My first encounters with the occult had struck a chord in me so deep I felt I would not be complete unless I could learn the meaning of that note.

"From whence do you come?"

"From the place of greatest darkness."

It was properly dark now, and silent except for the occasional pop and sparkle of my fire. I had a piece of oak branch across the top, and I turned it over to watch the sparks tumbling up and catch the extra heat from the glowing underside. I heard a crack that seemed to come from a distance away to my right, and quickly turned and stared into the darkness, but saw nothing. I felt suddenly alert though, and with some trepidation stood up as quietly as I could and listened with all my concentration. There were no more noises and I sat down again, feeling a bit foolish and just a little scared. What was I doing, exactly? I had no idea, although a month ago it had seemed like the opportunity of a lifetime when my friend had asked me if I wanted to join the group.

"You seem interested in all this occult stuff," he said. "If you really do want to learn magick, you should get initiated, get to know the other members and the kind of things we do. It's easy enough, you just have some words to say on cue, and then you take an oath of silence." My response had the enthusiasm of one who is stranded in the Gobi desert and who has been offered directions to the nearest oasis.

A few days later he told me that I would be expected to provide my own robe and gave me a photocopy of the script, from which I learned that I would be naked, blindfolded, and bound hand and foot but loosely so that I would be able to walk and get free if I wished. A week or two after that he asked me once more and finding my reply agreeable he gave me a date, "the week after Samhain." I quickly found out that I was due to be initiated into the Neophyte Grade of the Ordo Argentum Astrum in the first week of November, about a fortnight away.

Suddenly out of the darkness there came a shrill whooping cry, followed by a burst of laughter. Was that them? I did not dare speculate as the velvet silence closed in around the quickened beating of my heart. I was undeniably rattled, and the excited anticipation I had felt before was being replaced with an unpleasant sensation as of a boxful of butterflies where my abdomen should be, conveying a vague dread of the unknown which was awaiting me. I had lost all sense of time, but my fire was beginning to diminish and I had no more firewood. Surely they would not be long now? I could not very well go wandering off in the dark looking for fuel, so I built up what was left, occupying my fretful mind, and soon had a small but cheery blaze to crouch over.

Another loud crack! Over my left shoulder that time, followed by voices speaking in low tones, some distance away. My resolve had stiffened with mending the fire. Indeed, I was so pleased with it I had almost hoped that I would not be imminently disturbed, but the sound of the voices made me turn about and wish that they would hurry up. The huge silence descended again however, and my presence in the wood seemed the least significant thing under the stars.

"Are you ready?" A commanding voice crashed into my awareness like a clap of thunder. A figure in a white robe with the hood concealing the face stood in front of me, and as I got to my feet another, similarly clad, came along the path from behind me and picked up my bag. "I – yes, I am ready," I said, although I seemed to have been turned into jelly and my mind had emptied out leaving only a high little whisper, "this is it, you fool, this is it!" I started as a loud splashy hiss erupted behind me. The second figure had poured water on the fire and now replacing the lid, he dropped the bottle into the carrier bag.

"Follow," he said, and I recognised the voice of my friend and guide. The fire was out, there was nothing else for it but to follow, into the wood. After about twenty paces we stopped and I was told to strip. I made a bundle of my clothes and one of my companions took it from me, while the other bent down to tie the ends of a long strip of cloth round my ankles. "Your hands," he said, standing behind me, "and now, your eyes." The cloth was soft, and firmly tied to be secure without causing discomfort, and the gulp of panic as the blindfold went over my eyes suffused itself into my whole being and gave sharpness and strength to my intuitive senses. Hands pushed gently but firmly at my shoulders so that I had to turn round two or three times where I stood, and then my friend said again, "are you ready," and I nodded and whispered "yes, I am ready" at the darkness. Yes, I'm ready, I'm cold but I don't feel it, I'm sure I look undernourished but it doesn't matter, because I'm too frightened to care, but I know that this is right for me, this step into the unknown is the best thing I've ever done, and so yes, I am ready.

The tempest which had rocked my life in the late 1970's had washed me up at the door of the individual who brought me to my woodland crossroad. I came to know him as Brother Pan. He lived in three rooms on the ground floor of a fine Georgian town-house, and had something of a local reputation as an eccentric. His place was known as a good place to go and hear interesting music and look at occult literature: a somewhat bohemian household through which all sorts of interesting people passed, a refuge for those who wanted to crash, or get a Tarot reading, or smoke weed and discuss matters of religion, science, astrology, and the occult, all through the night hours till the dawn light crept in. There was glitter in the carpet and the lightbulbs were coloured green and red and purple; magic mushrooms would be on hand in season, drying in heaps on sheets of newspaper. The front room was kept locked and it was a matter of etiquette to pretend that it did not exist. That was understood. But there were hints of secret magic, nothing specific, just an unspoken awareness that there was more than met the eye happening in that house. It was there that my life's thread was woven into the fabric of English Qaballa, sometime in 1979 when I first encountered the *Book of the Law*.

The book was clearly hand-made, pages of photocopied typescript stapled together between light cardboard covers and the spine bound with cloth tape, interesting in itself, but all the words had numbers neatly typed underneath, and there were numbers throughout the text as well, which pricked my curiosity severely. I was immediately struck by the beauty of the language, the poetic imagery was strangely inspiring, and I wanted very much to read the whole text. One was welcome to browse through the magazines and books on witchcraft and astrology and Qabalah and Magick that lay scattered or in piles on the floor of Pan's living room, and to cut a longish story short, I became a frequent visitor.

Pan would not say what the significance of the numbers was, but was amused and indulgently happy for me to try and understand on my own. Over the course of a few days I read the whole thing and the impact on my teenage mind was like nothing else I had ever experienced from reading anything. I could not get my mind around the contrast between the beauty of the first chapter and the cruelty of the third: I felt scorched by the questions of how and why such opposing themes existed in the same document? The work struck a massively resonant chord in my psyche, seeming to speak to me directly, and I fervently wanted to know more.

My life up to that point had been middle-class ordinary on the outside hiding a desperately individual passion as yet undefined, expressed in a rebellious nature and a restless creativity. In those days I thought my artistic talent was the guiding light that my life would follow; it had cut me out from the herd at school and encouraged me to seek friendships with similarly outlaw characters, with whom I could spend hours talking and playing records or walking into the countryside to light a fire of twigs and smoke an unlawful roll-up or two. I knew no more of the occult than can be gleaned from the fiction of Dennis Wheatley; I had never heard of Aleister Crowley, and had only the vaguest notion of astrology. I considered myself a Christian – which is to say, I believed in Jesus – but found Christianity unsatisfactory as a system upon which to base my life.

Into these vaguely drifting mists of spiritual awareness there had come a vision of light that I could not quite catch hold of, a Siren-song whose tune I could not remember, when I first read *Liber AL*. I was hooked, I badly wanted to know more, and as I continued to pester my friend Pan to let me sit and ponder over the numbers and words it dawned on me that he and some of the other people I met at his house were members of a genuine occult group, who had produced this very text. They had also published one of the slew of occult magazines at Pan's, bound in the same fashion, called "The New Equinox/British Journal of Magick"; there were two or three editions, along with some QBLH pamphlets and something called "The Cincinnati Journal of Ceremonial Magick", memorable because it contained an article on how to draw a Tree of Life with compasses and a ruler.

One morning in the spring of 1980 I was sitting in one of Pan's armchairs, enveloped in that golden drowsiness that comes over one some time before midday when one has been up all night in the company of half a dozen psilocybin. There entered someone I had not seen before, wearing a 50's style corduroy jacket and wellington boots and smoking a curly black pipe, a Peterson, with the silver band. He came in and sat down with complete ease and familiarity, as if he'd been there all along and had just popped out for a moment, and Pan addressed him respectfully as 'Jim'. He said something to Pan about "this Sun Venus business," and they began a discussion that went straight through my semi-conscious doze and filled my mind with an image of startling clarity and light. When I woke I felt an overwhelming urge to rush home and paint my vision before it faded, fancying that it might be significant. It wasn't, but it did show promise, being a sort of Caduceus with a Zodiac wheel instead of the wings and disk. I was working with oils at the time, and when the paint was dry I offered the picture up for criticism. It was pronounced "interesting" and perhaps suitable for inclusion in the magazine.

Later on I was properly introduced to Jim Lees, who sat me down and asked me what I thought. The question threw me, as it was meant to; nobody had asked me for my thoughts before, and I cannot remember what sort of mumbled reply I came up with. He was very kind and patient, genuinely interested in discovering my motivational sources; he cast my horoscope and told me about myself.

In the years which followed I got to know a little about Jim's background and magickal work. He was born in Bolton, Lancashire, on August 22, 1939, and unlike the vast majority of people in the West, he retained the memory of being born, and where he was beforehand. Chemistry was a childhood passion, and Lees became an analytical chemist in one of the foremost metallurgical laboratories of the day; but the juxtaposition of his pre-birth memories with the experiences of his childhood in the grim poverty of 1940s Lancashire spurred him to ask the big questions – "Where did I come from, where am I going, what's the prize, and what are the rules?" He became preoccupied with the question of what would happen to him after his death, his unusual memories and a terrifying awareness of his own mortality presenting him with a terrible conflict, for human existence seemed catastrophic if there was only one life to live but quite a different proposition if reincarnation were truly involved.

He made a study of psychology according to Jung, Freud, Adler, and Lang, but found no satisfactory answers, and realised that science offered him no real solution, only more questions, as every rule has its anomalies and exceptions. Lees turned to Astrology and for a time made a living practising Horary Astrology, and became convinced that belief in the concept of a God who created the universe and populated it with inferior beings to watch them live and die and suffer for all eternity was quite untenable, a ludicrous state of affairs, with a miserably sadistic deity.

Lees found the mental and emotional torment of these questions intolerable and he resolved to discover the answers for himself. He conducted an intensive examination of the world's major religions and their mystical disciplines, looking for a system of meditation that would lead him to the Absolute Truth that he sought.

After much deliberation James Lees decided to use the Hebrew Kabbalah and the Tree of Life, in combination with the Yogic disciplines of Pranayama and Hathayoga. He was already familiar with the Hebraic magical tradition, his Astrological studies having led him to the invocation of planetary spirits using the Key of Solomon. Proving to his satisfaction that it worked, Lees went on to successfully complete the 18-month operation of the Abramelin system, including the proper performance of the Bornless Rite and following up with other rituals of Crowleyanity, and he mastered Bardon's Hermetic system of initiation. His work with the Hebrew Tree of Life was primarily informed by Israel Regardie's *Middle Pillar* and Dion Fortune's *Mystical*

Qabalah and continued for fifteen years, during which time he experienced all of the visions associated with the spheres on the Tree as his consciousness ascended the Middle Pillar, culminating in the Crossing of the Abyss and a final vision of Divine Truth, a spiritual attainment almost unheard of in the annals of mysticism.

Following this ultimate visionary experience, Lees wanted to find out if it was possible to help others on the same Quest for enlightenment. He wanted to know whether it was in fact possible to initiate any candidate into the Mysteries, as suggested in the teachings of the Golden Dawn. The group that he formed in 1974 with three friends was fairly informal to begin with; they met often to discuss Hebrew Kabbalah, Astrology, and other strands of Western Occultism.

I nearly met Jim in 1975 when my parents moved from the Hertfordshire of my childhood and bought a detached town house in need of some repair. Jim, who ran a plumbing and electrical business at the time, did some work there, but I was away at school. The group was just over a year old then, and Brother Pan was living in the woods where they did their witchcraft rituals. He had built a hut there and stayed in it through the winter and early Spring of 1976, until he got his ground floor apartments in town. The hut was left intact, and made use of by other, unknown people. In the long hot summer of that year a fire started in the woods and spread out of control. From my bedroom window across the valley I could see the flames as they rose above the tree tops. I did not guess or even suspect what those woods held in store for me just a few years later.

Fundamental Magickal Education

THERE WERE SEVEN other initiated members of the Order of the Silver Star, or O∴A∴A∴, when I joined the group. I already knew Brother Pan, who had been my Summoner; a bit taller than average, he was a big-boned Aquarian with disorderly brown wavy hair and a smile full of mischief, and a penchant for making fireworks and other madcap devices. I had met the Priestess who held office in the West: Sister Thelema, also known as Carol Smith, a blonde Piscean as lovely as Pamela Coleman Smith's portrait of the Empress in the Rider Tarot. She was largely responsible for the five issues of TNE/BJM, editing Jim's notes, doing the layouts, negotiating with the printers, looking after the mailing lists, and so on.

The High Priestess of the group was Sister Maat, a petite Libran beauty with long black hair and a ballerina's grace; a talented sculptor in clay, she looked every inch the Kundalini Witch that she actually was, and eminently suited for the position of Officer of the North. In the East stood Brother Thoth, Stefan Djanowicz; his Polish ancestry showing in his pale complexion and almost black hair and beard, he was slenderly built, intense, bespectacled and quietly spoken, and one of the best E. Qaballists in the group. The Guard was Brother Hermes, a more stocky individual with mousy-blond hair and blue eyes, a good astrologer and medium, who a year or two before had been the last initiate before me.

The chief was Brother Leo, Jim Lees, whom I had met a few times previously and who held the Sword while I took my Magickal Oath. Next to him stood Brother Hersechel, a tall and very Jovian-looking man, quick to laughter, with twinkly blue eyes and a broad moustache; possessing an encyclopaedic memory for astrological detail, he had everyone's natal and progressed astrology at his fingertips.

Jim Lees had the breadth of compassion reserved for those who have both witnessed and experienced the worst of hard times and great suffering. His intuitive skills were nothing short of brilliant and he could read people and situations instantly, accurately predicting the behaviour of individuals and the inevitable outcomes as easily as a chef dealing with a recipe book, and he was always ready to put his own interests last while he sought to enhance the lives of others. He had been studying and practising magick for over 20 years, self taught and self initiated and fully conversant with his Holy Guardian Angel and several other significant entities; he would say that he had found the answers to all of his questions, and lost his hair in the process. His wisdom and experience was wide and deep and given generously to whoever was in need of it, and not exclusively to the group either, for a number of uninitiated friends and acquaintances would drift in and out, bringing favours or small gifts or simply entertaining us in return. They all knew there were other things going on, but never asked awkward questions or spread idle gossip, and the group's existence was kept a close secret for nearly a decade.

On the bookshelves and mantelpieces, in the nooks and corners, if one cared to look, there were sheets of handmade paper, ingots of beeswax, ritual masks and magickal weapons, there were talismans of copper and tin, and Enochian tablets, and ritual jewelry, and statues of Egyptian deities, and all manner of occult paraphernalia hidden away in everyone's houses and apartments, all made by the members. Hersechel worked in a dental laboratory and made small silver castings for rings and talismans; he could acquire quantities of dental wax too, and for the woodland rituals Hersechel, Pan, and Leo would make huge wax torches that would last for hours. One night they drove home from a ritual with flaming torches protruding from the car windows and dripping molten wax spraying all over the bodywork. The marks never did come off.

Herbs were another area of interest, both medicinal and narcotic, and there were frequently substances available for testing. Expeditions were mounted in winter and summer to seek out coltsfoot and St. John's wort in the surrounding countryside. The former was an ingredient in cough medicine, and with the latter was made an ointment for burns which was an essential in all our kitchens. Sister Thelema made shampoo and hair rinse with soapwort; damiana was another popular infusion. There was proper witch's flying ointment, and witch's ink too, and psilocybin, and amanita muscaria, and cannabis, and miniature cubensis buttons, and various aphrodisiacs, including yohimbe and something supposed to be rhinoceros horn, all subjected to our researches. Brother Leo would require detailed accounts of experiences, always cautioning and advising, and when necessary (but this was rare) mending.

We all lived within a thirty mile radius, and met every weekend and throughout the week too, in and out of each-other's houses to help with domestic projects, or to discuss the latest occult idea, or share the latest acquisition of literature or music or intoxicant, or just for a chat and a cup of tea. Brother Leo kept an eye on us all as we ran about, and gently gathered us all up so that we moved as one towards the performance of the next ritual. The English Qaballa and its application to the *Book of the Law* was our continuous point of focus, the words and the numbers energizing our conversations and occupying our thoughts.

Not long after my initiation Jim showed me how to read an Ephemeris and draw a simple astrological chart, encouraging me to practise horary astrology. He entrusted his copies of Regardie's *Middle Pillar* and Fortune's *Mystical Qabalah* to me, and helped me with the Lesser Banishing Pentagram Rite and the meditations as I began daily performance of those exercises, using rhythmic breathing and relaxation for 20 minutes to start with, and extending the meditation time eventually to 90 minutes. Being handy with drawing instruments, pen and ink, watercolour, and other tools of the fine art studio, I soon had a large diagram of the Hebrew Tree of Life, fully annotated and coloured from the descriptions given by Dion Fortune and from Crowley's *777*. I copied tables of correspondences for the 22 paths, complete with Tarot interpretations, and also copied out the attributions and rulerships of astrology. And most of all I had my very own enumerated copy of the *Book of the Law* and its Comment, with its index of numbers and their words and the reproduction of the manuscript.

It was accepted practice within the group to annotate our copies of AL: if we found two or more words whose total value was of interest we would write the numbers underneath, with arrows or just short diagonal lines to show which words had been added. This work had been going on for some time before I joined, and a lot of numbers had been found and shared within the group, so that they had become a kind of conversational shorthand. Jim paid me the huge compliment of allowing me to take his enumerated *Liber AL* home so that I could catch up by copying his work, which I completed in a one long session.

I learned the E. Qaballistic technique of reading words and numbers all at once, a double-reading on two lines at the same time, which has the eventual effect of turning the words to heiroglyphs, and the numbers to a clear language of symbols, fluidic and quite ungrammatical. Our home-made copies of *AL* became dog-eared with use and heavily annotated with the scribbled values of pairs or small sequences of words, astrological and alchemical symbols, inspired notes, and so forth. We would go away and work alone with a set of words and values, and at the frequent group meetings we would share our latest "bits of E.Q." and discuss our conclusions. We could draw on a wide and deep collective pool of knowledge and experience of a range of subjects including astrology, chemistry, physics, Hebrew Kabbalah, Crowleyanity, the Papers of the Golden Dawn, Witchcraft, Goetia, mythology, yoga, European history, horticulture, alchemy, metallurgy, engineering, and the major religions and mystical systems of the world.

Jim's bookshelves held the volumes of Crowley's *Equinox* and Blavatsky's *Secret Doctrine* and Bardon's *Hermetica*, and works by W.G. Gray and A.E. Waite and Gershom Scholem and Kenneth Grant, by Dion Fortune and Frances Yates and Israel Regardie and John Allegro and Paul Huson and Oliver Lodge, and many books on astrology, on mysticism and astral travel and dreamlore and ley-lines and sex-magic and Tarot; he had a first edition Thoth Tarot, and a number of the books had been inscribed or signed by the author. My inclination obviously leaning towards mysticism, he suggested Scholem and Gray, both of whom impressed me greatly; I peeped into Blavatsky but decided I wasn't old enough to explore that territory. Crowley I found occasionally brilliant, but heavy going for the most part, preferring the more kindly style of Regardie. I read as much and as widely as I could manage, and for a long time I thought of little else but English Qaballa and *Liber AL*, astrology, and Hebrew Kabbalah.

I was at least ten years younger than anyone else, and I had a lot of catching up to do in terms of simply learning the basics, the symbols and God-Names and colours and so forth. I studied Astrology and Hebrew Kabbalah simultaneously, through the lens of English Qaballa, for at the heart of my personal Quest was the longing to understand what *Liber AL* meant and why it seemed to speak so intimately to me. At group meetings I mostly sat quiet and spongelike, absorbing as much as I could, and often would write up what I could remember of the discussions when I got home.

The work was two-fold, involving analysis and then synthesis, when we took our conclusions and tested them against available knowledge from everywhere and anywhere, anything and everything, looking for reflections in other spheres to prove or disprove the accuracy and usefulness of the idea. Jim made a speciality of E. Qaballistic synthesis, and made us all attempt to realise our conclusions on different planes and in different areas of the human psyche. "It's no use as a formula if you can't apply it to anything else," he would say. "Nothing happens in isolation."

Often there would be a word or a phrase in *Liber AL* that pointed to a specific magical or occult idea or symbol, which would be added up and its number checked. E.Q. does not so much bring new ideas to the table as thoroughly clean up old ideas, and then it presents them in a new way, the numeric correspondences making links between them that are new and pure and irrefutable, being based on numbers which cannot be anything other than what they are. English Qaballists experience a kind of continuous wave-surfing Eureka moment, such is the energy evoked in qaballistic revelation; it is an ecstasy of mind, a soaring joy, led on by numbers that do not lie or play tricks. We were like children stringing beads of exotic light, wandering in a treasure-house that had never been lit before, as symbols and archetypes came smoothly together by the power of their numbers. It was like the best contact high of all time.

"Follow the numbers!" we would remind each other: words that rang like a battle-cry sometimes as we surged ahead. We knew our minds were being stretched and moulded but we didn't care, it was a joyous experience. Questions were being answered properly, problems were resolved and settled, and there was nothing left over that had to be fudged or ignored.

It made the very air sparkle sometimes, for we were invoking old ideas by new names and under different powers into this fascinating matrix of numbers which was emerging in our shared consciousness. It was hugely exciting, compelling, even addictive; oh, the energy! being so new and vibrant and rising on its own vortex! the atmosphere fairly crackled with it some nights. Jim with his experience and wisdom was our guide in this new inner landscape we were building. He scaled the mountain while we followed closely, widening the path and making maps.

Often the numbers would pop out again later and catch us unawares; in the shop the cashier sings out the digits we had been riding with earlier the same day, and inevitably this makes us laugh, and feel a mixture of awe and appreciation, and say things like, "Well, of course, it would have to be that!" and, "No surprises there!" or just, "Oh!" The spirit of English Qaballa is quite the jester.

It was inspiring, and somewhat scary. "Feel secure in it all, do you?" Jim asked me a few days after my first Pentagram Ritual had all but knocked me off my feet. "Well, sort of," I said. "It's the only show in town," he said, "you're like someone who's woken up on a train and you don't know where you came from, still less where you're going. You have to grab that tiger by the tail, and hang on! – but you'll be all right," he added with a quick smile, "the Powers That Be never give you more than you can handle." I was glad of the reassurance, then as now; I was in the grip of an urgent overwhelming desire and need to know that conquered my uncertainties and drove me on.

I made myself useful in other ways, contributing some illustrations to the *New Equinox/British Journal of Magick* and helping with the collating of the pages when they returned from the printer's. I could sew, and I could type, and did so willingly, and I made tea and washed up, and counted myself the luckiest of young women to be living such a fabulous adventure. One day Jim asked me if I'd ever done any sculpture, and when I regretfully replied that I wasn't very good at the three-dimensional, he suggested bas-relief. "You could make a Stele of Revealing," he said.

I accepted the challenge with excitement. I went home, and carefully cast a block of finishing plaster two inches thick and thirteen by twenty-two inches. I bought a small sharp kitchen knife, and Brother Hersechel gave me a dental technician's tool with a blunt end and an offset chisel edge, which was very useful. I also used a darning needle, and an old treasured penknife. I scaled up the design of the Stele in the usual way, drawing it out on the plaster with a pencil, and began carving at the top, finding the curve of the Goddess's arched back.

As a figurative artist I was accustomed to the negotiations that go on between the image and the hand, with the forces that come in through the eyes and out through the fingers. I was used to communicating and sharing and identifying with my subject to the exclusion of all else, in the effort of reproducing what it felt like. So I naturally invoked the lambent flame of Nuit, the Queen of the Stars. I invoked Hadit as I carved the winged disk and the hieroglyphs. I invoked Horus of the Hawk's Head while I worked on the figure of the enthroned God, and I invoked the Priest Ankh-af-na-Khonsu standing in his leopardskin cloak with his arm outstretched. I identified with each of them, and as I carved the hieroglyphs underneath I began to understand the meaning of the ritual. I filled my bedsit with plaster-dust. I had to put a bracer on my right wrist; I worked until I was exhausted. Once a tiny chip flew up to my eye from the plaster surface; I saw it take off from the knife-point and rise in a slow arc, and I had plenty of time to blink and feel it bounce off my eyelid. I slept when I had to, and when I woke I went back to work, grudging the time used for eating and other necessities. My Muse was driving me hard.

The work took a fortnight, and was finished in time for the three day celebration of the Writing of the *Book of the Law*. I made up a rite, and consecrated the Knife I had used upon the Stele. I had been following the sequence delineated in the "Spell Called the Sky" and with my red flame of a Knife I made my secret door, and the Light consumed me. There followed a period in which I seemed to be enveloped in cotton wool of the softest pinkish-gold kind. I had embodied the Ritual of the Stele and awakened the Self-Slain Prince-Priest, baring my breast before the Altar of Horus and pouring out my devotion to Nuit with all my naive little bits of skill and strength. What I learned has to do with sacrifice.

Drying in the sun; Stele of Revealing carved and painted by Cath Thompson.

Apposite Biographical Interlude

The story of the O∴A∴A∴ up to the time of my initiation was straightforward enough. Jim Lees formed the group in 1974 with three friends who were interested in learning about the occult. They found a woodland glade a few miles away, isolated, and large enough for them to consecrate a Circle there, and under his guidance they began practising seasonal and wiccan rituals. They took Magickal names and learned techniques of invocation and evocation and meditation, the making of talismans, ritual procedure and temple etiquette mostly along Golden Dawn lines, with bits of witchcraft and Crowleyanity thrown in. Lees shared his occult library and his experience with the group, and when in later years they acquired an indoor Temple and three more members they extended their work to include the Rites of Eleusis written by Aleister Crowley, which they performed in full, and a study of the Enochian system.

In February 1976 Lees began a nine-month magickal retirement at the instruction of his Angel: the command was to "Remain Silent". He performed banishing rituals and the Bornless Ritual again, and he noted that every magickal endeavour and operation that he undertook came easily to him, presenting no challenges whatsoever. Eventually, towards the end of his retirement, Lees' attention was drawn to *Liber AL vel Legis*, that most mysterious and obscure of occult texts. Being well versed in Hebrew gematria he began to experiment with letters and numbers, and when the other three members of the group came round they naturally joined in, for it was late

November, the 26th in fact, and there wasn't much going on. They homed in on the sequence of letters and numbers in AL II:76 with pens and pencils and sheets of paper, and somehow all four separate sets of calculations came up with the number 286, "the wrong result," Lees noted later, "but the right answer as far as *AL* was concerned." Lees knew that 286 was significant, insofar as being the sum of 22x13 it reflected the 22 letters of the Hebrew Alphabet and the emphasis on the Moon in Judaism.

But there was more. 286 is also the sum of 26x11, which indicated the 26 letters of the English Alphabet and an association with the number 11, which was mentioned more than once in *Liber AL*.

Lees reasoned that if the 13 indicated a key to the Hebrew Alphabetical system, then 11 might be the Key to the English. He counted off every eleventh letter of the English Alphabet, leaving 'A' with the value 1. This gave the sequence A=1, L=2, W=3, H=4, S=5, D=6, O=7, Z=8, K=9, V=10, G=11, R=12, C=13, N=14, Y=15, J=16, U=17, F=18, Q=19, B=20, M=21, X=22, I=23, T=24, E=25, P=26. There was some work with calculators as all four occultists began adding up names and important words from *Liber AL*. Lists of words of the same value started to form and they looked for any correlation between words of equal value, to find whether there were any common threads, or any corresponding symbols.

And there were.

Every letter became a bold and disturbing numeric symbol. They also found that this new order and value of the English Alphabet produced a unicursal 26-pointed star, which was very satisfying. (Some years later Jake Stratton-Kent found a second unicursal 26-pointed star which returned the Qaballistic Order and Value of the letters to that of the common alphabet.)

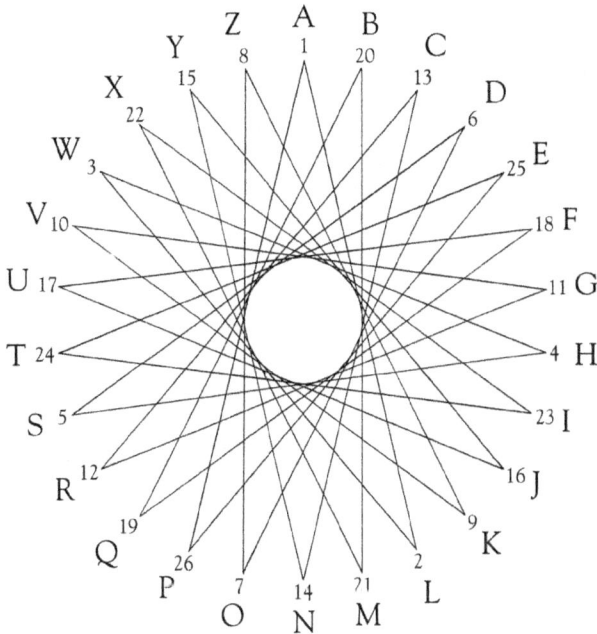

More significant later on was the discovery that it had been encoded in the manuscript all along, on Sheet 16 of the third day's dictated handwriting in Crowley's notebook; the inexplicable grid on that page gives the Key when one fills in the common alphabet in columns from "A" in the top left corner. The Qaballistic Order and Value then appear on the diagonal as indicated in the text, "... then this line drawn is a key....and Abrahadabra." (AL III:47). Abrahadabra is a word of 11 letters, another pointer towards the Key.

Furthermore, the diagram itself is a map of the location of the discovery of the Key. The line drawn is in actuality a public road; the circle squared represents an area which had been named Rosy Cross by some unknown property dealer who bought the land after a successful bet on a race horse of that name, and Lees' home where the Key was discovered is in the position of the word "whence" upon the grid.

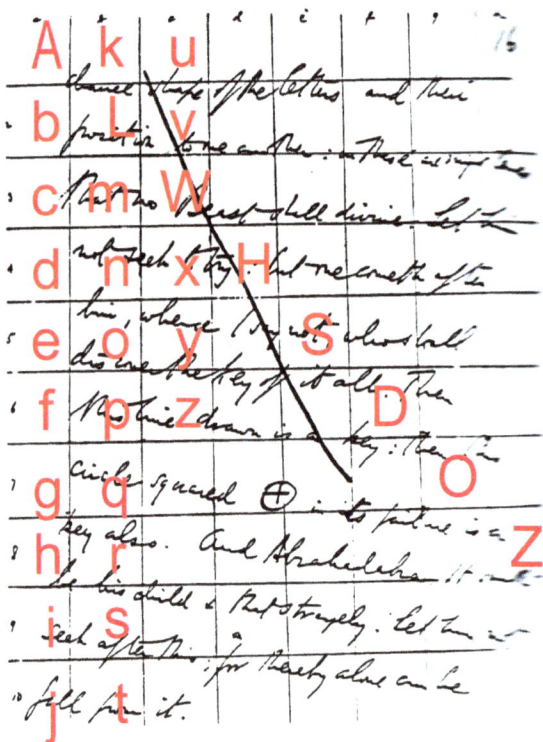

ALL THIS AND A BOOK

It was clear to all four that something of great import was happening. Lees named his occult group Ordo Argentum Astrum, and they began to investigate the new enumeration. Over the next few days there was a lot of feverish working at calculators and writing of hasty notes as it became undeniable that the correspondences lined up. The numbers 11 and 76 recurred with the date, they noticed, the twenty-sixth day standing for the 26 letters and the eleventh month for the Key number 11, and the seventy-sixth year for the verse which gave the Key, 76. Moreover the chapter and verse numerals 2:76 may be written 11:76 which also means November 1976.

To add to the drama the mains electricity supply to Lees' home became quite erratic for the next day or two, causing household appliances to go slow or speed up, lights to dim and brighten, and so forth. It was all very exciting.

The value of every word, phrase, sentence, and verse in the *Book of the Law* was worked out (pocket calculators had come on the market just in time for this labourious task) and an enumerated typescript of the text and its Comment, with the required reproduction of the original manuscript, was painstakingly prepared and photocopied, collated, stapled between lightweight cardboard covers and bound with cloth tape, by and for the members.

Lees christened the new alphabet "English Qaballa" having made sure no-one else was using that particular spelling in 1976. He wrote to Kenneth Grant, thinking that the OTO ought to be informed, but Grant replied that he couldn't see the point of a qabalah in English. Israel Regardie was not comfortable with the new attributions either – why does D correspond with 6, he wondered. Only

William Webb of QBLH responded, some time later, with any spark of interest.

So Lees, and his group, worked alone at the development of the new Qaballa. Words of the same value resonated the same ideas, and Lees soon realised that the names of the planets and Zodiac Signs also synchronised through their numbers with other symbols. Moreover, the traditional methods of Gematria worked with the English Qaballa, and there was no outrage done to any existing system. For instance, 7 was the number of Venus, but as the E.Q. value of the letter "O" it revealed something more about the virginal purity of the goddess, not least because O is also 0 or Zero, which is Nothing. Words could also be analysed by examining their component letters: GOD for example, can be read as GO, D. The letter D has the numerical value 6 which is the value of LAW and by synthesising GO and LAW we come to an understanding of God as the principle of Motion which resonates nicely with Newtonian physics and with Crowley's idea that "one's function is to Go."

Lees noticed that the value of ABRAHADABRA (=79) was the reverse of the value of RA HOOR KHUT (=97), and AL III:1 calls the former the "reward" of the latter; and so it followed that the reversal of a word's numeric value would give the value of the reward of that word. So the reward of GOD=24 is 42=CROSS (the Elements and the basis of Manifestation) and 42=STAR (reiterating the same idea again in a more refined sense) and 42=BLOOD (which again resonates a profoundly similar concept, enhanced when we remember that the DNA molecule presents a Cross in a circle when viewed endways).

In the weeks following the discovery of the Key, instructions given in the text for its calculation became clear. With hindsight AL I:36, "My scribe Ankh-af-na-Khonsu, the priest of the princes, shall not in one letter change this book," and AL I:54, "Change not as much as the style of a letter," quite literally demand that all letters except 'A' should be changed. The number eleven is mentioned in *Liber AL* with emphasis, "My number is 11, as all their numbers who are of us," (I:60) and "as my bride is eleven" (II:16), suggesting the particular significance of the number; nevertheless, the Key to the Qaballa was obtained without recourse to this sort of logic.

At the end of the 1970's Lees considered the research into the English Qaballa and its application to the *Book of the Law* sufficiently conclusive and interesting to be put before the occult reading public. In 1980 Kaaba Publications was established to make available the essential details of the new system, and over the next two years Jim Lees and Carol Smith edited and published five issues of the magazine *The New Equinox: The British Journal of Magick*. The title was taken over from Ray Sherwin who, in his final edition of the magazine, published the first short article about English Qaballa, worked up from notes given to him by Lees. Sherwin contributed another article or two worked up from Lees' notes, and Lees wrote many essays which were edited by Carol Smith and published under an assortment of different by-lines. (In later years this in-joke was misunderstood and taken seriously, but even an inexpert analysis of writing style is sufficient to demonstrate the authenticity of Lees' authorship of the articles dealing with E.Q.). Lees had at least twelve good years training and experience over anyone else and he defined all of the methods of English Qaballa apart from "Counting Well" which was worked out by Stefan Djanowicz.

Lees and Smith published 250 copies of each edition, and they went all over the world; letters came back from Australia and India and Poland and America and Japan and Canada. A young occultist named Jake Stratton-Kent wrote a good letter and submitted an article on the Lemegeton, both pieces appearing in TNE/BJM volume 2; some years later Lees handed the magazine format on to him and he published several more editions under the title *The Equinox/British Journal of Thelema.*

Stratton-Kent met Lees shortly before I came on the scene, and I first met him soon after. He visited our group on a number of occasions in the early 1980's, most often staying at Lees' house, where sometimes he would nip off upstairs to do a Bornless Rite or some other demonic invocation. Stratton-Kent was a wiry, eccentric, brown-eyed, elfin-faced sorcerer of medium height, clean-shaven, and in those days he was bald save for a little Thelemic tuft at the front of his head. He had his own small occult group in the West Country and was keen to spread the new Qaballa amongst his neophytes, and we were enthusiastic about their affiliation to our cause. Our *modus operandi* was more or less scientific; every move we made was rigorously tested at the theoretical stage as well as the practical, and the more data we could add the more sure we could be before we took the next risk with our sanity. And if things went wrong the damage could more easily be limited if it were more thinly spread than if it focussed on just a few.

There was also the idea that individuals were drawn to the group, that they were "meant to be there" to contribute what they might, and take from us what we had to give. It appeared that we were all on the same path, perhaps on parallel lines, and at different stages of learning and experience and enlightenment. People who have experienced the terrors of the 32nd Path can recognise the fear, or the resolution of it, in others.

Furthermore, Lees was interested in the initiatory process and whether it was indeed possible to initiate an individual through ritual alone, whether exposure to the forces employed in a Neophyte initiation would permanently alter the individual's psyche and cause consciousness expansion and subsequent modification of the personality, or whether it would merely awaken hitherto dormant factors which if left un-nourished would simply fade away again over a relatively short time. Then there was the notion of collective initiation, something of which the group had experienced in the culmination of the Eleusian Cycle and which seemed eminently possible, especially if there were other factors involved beyond the Neophyte ceremony.

As the group membership swelled in the 1980's it became clear that not only was it a question of the candidate's innate spiritual/magickal abilities, but also a question of timing, the astrological theory underlying the proposition being that everything partakes of the nature of its moment of birth. The aim of initiation is the alchemy of refinement, to balance and harmonise the candidate and render him or her a fit vessel for "higher" magickal/spiritual forces to indwell, therefore the ritual would be most appropriately designed to synchronise with an initiatory astrological configuration to get the cosmos involved from the beginning. Such a ceremony could potentially initiate the entire convocation of ritualists.

There are all sorts of different reasons why the conjunction of the Sun and Venus is the time for Initiation. Astronomically the positions of the conjunctions form a pentagram around the Earth roughly once every eight years. The Rosicrucian symbolism of the marriage between the Lord and the Lady needs no further elucidation. Traditionally Venus contains all the planets, and in astrological terms the solar conjunction is a combustion of planetary force; in astro-magickal terms, the sun at dawn is suffused in the refulgent Grail-Cup of Isis-Fortuna-Babalon. There is a window of time therefore when the celestial power of the Company of Heaven may be mediated with a minimum of interference. Lees applied the English Qaballa to these astrological principles and his hypothesis gained strength and credibility.

SUN = 36 + VENUS = 71 = 107 which is the value of MAGICIAN, meaning that a Magician is one who has accomplished the union of the Rose and the Cross within his own psyche and harmonised himself with the Cosmos to such an extent that he is able to mediate the Stellar influences at the point of the pentagram.

107 is the value of SILENCE, a quality which really is a Magickal Virtue as indicated in the Hermetic axiom "To Know, To Dare, To Will, and To Keep Silent – and the greatest of these is Silence." This does not constitute a ban on discussion nor promote secrecy *per se*; but it does have relevance to the kinds of magickal experiences of enlightenment which occur on planes of consciousness beyond or higher than rational thought. Those events are literally beyond description and tend to boggle and blow the mind all out of shape until they have properly assimilated the psyche, and it is a mistake to try and squash

the enormity of the vision into words too soon; better to gently allow these things to earth themselves than to interfere by attempting to hurry them along with premature analysis. And sometimes we require our magick to remain unearthed, in which instance we must not speak of it, ever. As *Liber AL* III:42 says, "Talk not overmuch!"

SUN=36 + AND=21 + VENUS=71 = 128 which is the value of THE ORDEAL X, a specific experience mentioned in AL III:22: "...the winners of the Ordeal X." Initiation involves ordeal; the shape of the letter X implicates the Cross as particularly characteristic of the 128 initiation. When the Candidate signs up for this he or she had better prepare to be shown everything that they are, set against everything that they are Not.

The digits of the number mean the Unity(1) of Duality(2) to, or in, Infinity(8). The epitome of duality is BAPHOMET, whose value just happens to be 128. This conglomerate entity is all dualities: Light and Dark, Solve and Coagula, Beast and Human, Bird and Fish, Devil and God. But the Double Serpents coil around a single Wand rising above the promise of the Rainbow, pointing ever upwards to the one crowning Light between the horns: Eliphas Levi's image of Baphomet shows us a balanced harmony of duality and thus symbolises a state of being that is attainable through THE ORDEAL X = BAPHOMET.

128 is the value of SCARLET WOMAN and that is the archetype that goes to work in the female psyche to accomplish the initiation: SCARLET=82=BALANCED, therefore this entity symbolises the state of Energy (represented by the colour) in Equilibrium. 82 is also the reward of 28 which is the value of HOLY and WORD,

meaning that She is capable of speaking a Word as a Master of the Temple and Winner of the Ordeal X.

ORDEAL X = 75 which is the value of THE BEAST. The component letters of the word BEAST can be written BE AS T and because T=24=GOD it can be read as an injunction to "Be as God" – or to "Be Ast (Isis)" – and here the letters AST = 1+5+24 = 30 = WILL. The Ordeal X then is capable of taking the candidate as far as the aspiration can reach.

The conclusion was that the celebration of a conjunction between the Sun and Venus, properly observed, should automatically begin the initiatory experience of the Ordeal X for all the celebrants at once. Early experiments tended to confirm this, with members recording similar kinds of mental and emotional upheavals, and dreams.

Also becoming clearer was the initiatory power of the *Book of the Law* and its Qaballa. Lees noted that "The initiatory teaching of the *Book of the Law* is not in the words but in the E.Qaballist's reaction to them. The first test is in the first reading. Then the reader will always find a proposition that will challenge him in some intimate way, when he will either discard it or find his curiosity aroused. It is no ordinary dead-letter text, it is not possible to judge it; it is alive, and it creates a dialogue with the student. It sets to work rather like a computer program to find out if he or she is worthy to understand any of its mysteries. The correspondences of the English Qaballa, the text of *AL*, the symbols and the numbers, infuse themselves into the conscious and unconscious mind, and the teaching is not in the words but in one's reactions to them. It may begin by testing one's moral integrity, presenting a proposition which seems untenable, or it may have a go at one's religious sensibilities or attack one's principles. Basic honesty is tested again and again to see if the student will try to bend the numbers to fit an idea, or attempt to twist an uneasy concept into something more palatable. There are times when one discards the work in disgust, only to be lured back into the drama by apparent coincidences. There are times when *AL*'s undoubted divine sense of humour turns up the same number repeatedly with guffaws of hilarity all round, and there are occasions when a string of ideas suddenly line up together in one's mind like the wheels in a one-armed bandit and one wins the jackpot of sublime enlightenment and ecstasy.

"The dedicated student will find his life altered by unseen hands. *Liber AL* will interact with every part of his being, it interrupts the working of the Soul sometimes with subtlety, sometimes with a savagery that he will barely withstand, creating the ordeals necessary for him to understand the secrets concealed within its text. Failure is an indication of the system highlighting an aspect of the student's psyche that he cannot cope with."

What was needed now was a full group ritual designed for Sun-Priest and Venus-Priestess with assistants and assembled worshippers. We discussed logistics, and we found a Sun-Venus in the spring of 1981, and Lees contacted Jake Stratton-Kent in case he might be interested in partaking in this endeavour.

Down in the West Country Stratton-Kent seemed enthusiastically inclined to ally his group, which was on the point of increasing its membership, with ours. It was thus agreed that this alliance should be recognised with a joint ritual which would have an additional initiating effect if all went according to plan, and we were invited to make use of his home and Temple for the purpose.

Precipitate Scandinavian Inflammation

WE SET OUT on one of those crisp April mornings, three Priestesses and four magickian-consorts in two cars, well supplied with flasks of coffee and packets of sandwiches and other dainties. The journey was uneventful and we found Jake's house easily enough and mooring space for the vehicles. We were expecting to find within some old friends and to be introduced to enthusiastic newly initiated occultists. Lively conversation, we thought as we disembarked, fresh tea, we anticipated, and maybe even entertainment. At any rate, as arranged, later on there would be the proper celebration of the conjunction of the celestial deities, followed by an appropriate feast. It had been a long journey, and we had quite forgotten that the planning stage of this event had occurred with the Moon in Scorpio.

The front door was opened after a pause by a somewhat dishevelled young man, bare-footed and blinking uncertainly in the early afternoon daylight. He beckoned us in with the surprised expression of one who finds himself welcoming a small crowd of total strangers into someone else's home. At the far end of the hallway a shadowy figure peeped out from a doorway. I glimpsed a flight of stairs leading to a landing from which encouraging noises were emerging, as we were shown into a living room on the left, where a large Alsatian dog lay snoozing in the corner. We sat and waited, and then our host appeared, energetically welcoming us and apologising for his Doorkeeper. There had been several initiations the night before, and a generous post-ritual celebration. We three visiting Priestesses found our way to the kitchen to assist with organising some refreshment and with introductions complete and cups of tea or coffee all round, everybody settled down in the living room and we carefully began to describe the kind of ritual we had planned, what we wanted to do and what was expected from the new members.

There would be the usual banishings and purifications, preliminary invocations of the Sun and of Venus, and the Identification of the High Priestess with the Goddess, and then the whole group would join in the adoration and worship of the Goddess in the body of the High Priestess with a simple chant.

Our audience grasped the all-important fact that they would not have to actually do anything that was beyond their somewhat hungover condition. A feast was arranged for consumption after the Temple ritual, and more wine was procured. The time for conversation ran its course. We robed up, and since the upstairs Temple room was not overly spacious we waited while an Officer of Jake's group performed the customary preliminaries, and then entered and took our places.

There was a low dais in the East, with a throne for the High Priestess, and a huge Pentagram banner hanging ceiling-to-floor behind. In the South-west, near the door, there was a gas fire of the glowing radiant variety, turned on low against the chilly April air, and already adding appreciable warmth. We sat on the floor in a rough semi-circle in front of the dais. The ritual proceeded in an orderly fashion and the room got hotter. Our thurible was pouring out the incense smoke, and there were a dozen of us beginning to chant in that heady atmosphere, calling forth the Beauteous One and starting the vortex of energy spinning around the close room.

Suddenly there came a low moaning sound, out of rhythm and noticeably lacking in enthusiasm. Through the wreathing clouds of benzoin and olibanum I recognised the tall heavily built shape of one of the newly initiated as it heaved and wobbled upwards toward the vertical, apparently in some distress. He had been introduced earlier as Brother Tyr and I remembered Icelandic grey eyes and tousled blondish hair, a liking for the Norse Gods and the physical build to match, and indeed he looked as if he was emerging from Valhalla after a particularly boisterous night's indulgence. The chanting stopped, and I watched, fascinated, as Tyr found both of his feet simultaneously and tried to make them work as Nature intended. He was facing the High Priestess, who had been standing as she received the adoring invocation of Venus, and who had unceremoniously sat down at the interruption. As he toppled towards her Brother Tyr tripped over the dais, and reaching out he clawed at the pentagram banner for support. The fabric was not equal to the task and gave way with a crash, and the High Priestess rose disdainfully from her throne and moved to one side to give him more room. Narrowly escaping the folds of cloth, he managed to remain upright and holding fast to his original intention he turned and aimed at the door again. This time he only missed by a couple of feet, collided with the wall and fell sideways, gently brushing his head against the gas fire on the way down and giving out an acrid crackle of singeing hair. He recovered bravely and managed another step or two before giving up the unequal struggle with a sigh and in the manner of a falling tree submitting to gravity he went down for the last time. In the silence I heard an unforgettable sound as his head bounced, twice, and I knew he'd finished. For a moment all was still save for the wisps of smoke idly curling from his unconscious pate.

Brother Tyr was only mildly concussed, there was no permanent damage in any department, and our High Priestess recovered her Libran composure almost immediately. Thus the ritual ended, and the tale of the Flaming Viking was born. The rest of the evening proceeded according to plan, the ritual observances were rightly performed, and, satisfied with the entertainment and having assured ourselves that the lad was unharmed, we packed up and headed for home, hungry but in high spirits, having witnessed a legend in the making.

I began to realise that there was a lot of humour in the occult, which was reflected in the magazines, and that it was not necessarily as complicated as it first appeared. The group customarily performed W.G. Gray's Seasonal Rituals and in the build-up to each one there would be heated discussions about rewriting some of the phrases which we knew would make us giggle, but we always concluded that no words could be changed, and once again Brother Thoth would have to intone "The Great Germinator" with a straight face. There were a number of W.G. Gray books on Jim's shelves and I found his writing very accessible and helpful as I worked to assimilate the basic knowledge of the Western Occult Tradition. In later years I was able to see that the difficulty with the Seasonal Rites lies in their lack of intrinsic focus.

The O∴A∴A∴ continued to explore the notion of astrologically timed rituals. With hindsight we observed that our April Sun conjunct Venus was also conjunct Mars, which accounted for the event of the Flaming Viking. There were more planetary configurations involving Venus, Jupiter, Mars, and Mercury which we were able to mark with ritual, and we learned how to use lunar aspects to reflect the planetary forces more precisely. The challenge was to make a particular moment prominent with significance, to exaggerate it and celebrate it, and to this end we developed a penchant for planetary feasting. *Liber AL* says "Feast! ... drink sweet wines and wines that foam!" and encourages a delicacy of excess; champagne was therefore on the menu, and many cream cakes. These confections were abundantly supplied by a local baker who would fill a couple of the shop window trays for us with eclairs and choux buns and vanilla slices and cream horns and apple turnovers and doughnuts. The meat would be barbecued, or cooked in advance, and sometimes we had a first course of salad hors d'oeuvre with quail's eggs or crab meat or salmon, and French bread; sometimes there would be fruit, or a cheese board, and chocolates and liqueurs to finish. We would take up a collection for these occasions, and I became group treasurer and kept the account with the fund in an old tin cashbox. Champagne was always the preferred beverage, and inebriation was supplemented with joints passing round. Summer was the favourite season for such events when we would assemble in someone's garden. All would be blessed and consecrated, rugs would be spread on the lawn and we ate with our hands from paper plates to save on washing up, and threw the chicken bones into the hedges.

On the appointed day we would meet early and get as much preparation done as we could, the main courses went into the oven or were arranged for barbecueing over oak charcoal, and pans of vegetables or rice would be prepared and ready for action. We would robe up and enter the Temple or outdoor Circle and begin the rite in the usual way, and at the agreed time we would take the smoking thurible to the dining area and continue around a suitably furnished table, or sit on the ground to one side of the balefire. There would be appetisers while we waited for the main feast, and a couple of champagne corks would be popped and we would drink a series of toasts. These were always the same: the first would always be "The Queen, God bless 'er!" for we maintained the traditional English occultist's allegiance to the Crown. Then we drank to the glory of the stars, to the cooks, and to absent friends and to each other, and someone would always remember to stand and propose the toasts to "Admiral Lord Nelson!" and to "Uncle Aleister – wherever he may be!" We found it best to get the work of invocations and consecrations done before feasting commenced; the rite would be closed with a cup of wine shared between the celebrants. The presiding Priest would pour the wine (vintage port was the preference) and the Priestess would bless it and offer the Cup to the Priest with the words, "Do what thou wilt shall be the whole of the Law." He would answer, "Love is the Law, Love under Will," before drinking and handing the Cup back to her, and saying, "There is no part of me that is not of the Gods!" The Priestess bore the Cup to each member in turn, and uttering the same words all would drink, careful to make sure that there would be a sufficient quantity remaining for her to make the last salutation.

We also began to take note of the way that odd things happened to events planned when the Moon was in the Burning Way, the misfortunate portion of the

Zodiac between 15 degrees Libra and 15 degrees Scorpio, so that the expected outcome was far from what actually happened, the April ritual being a good example. In the English Qaballa SCORPIO has the same value as ENDING and DIVIDE, good words for the traditional astrological House of Death, while Libra signifies the Judgement which precedes the final departure: events cannot be predicted using the Horary method with the Moon in the Burning Way. On the international stage we watched the negotiations for the handover of Hong Kong tending to coincide with the Moon being in Scorpio, and later it was clear that while the world had expected the strict Chinese regime to impose itself on the island, Scorpio reversed the direction of power and it was the capitalist consumerism of Hong Kong that swept into the mainland. From this we also learned that Scorpio had a way of keeping records of new ideas and themes, and when the time came around the file would be opened and we would find ourselves making the same plans and having the same conversations as we had the previous month.

We noticed Scorpio at work in our post Sun-Venus experiences too, as we all individually and collectively entered into the Ordeal X. We noted an initial unity of purpose within the group, suddenly exploded by behavioural changes leading inevitably to estrangement and irrational hostility, as individual members came under the pressure of division into Self and Not-Self. This internal conflict can become obsessive; to survive one must recognise this phenomenon and deal with it. The way in which one does so defines whether one passes that part of the Ordeal or not. The results can be ruinous, as happened within Crowley's organisation and its successors; Jim wrote "that the force was 93 there is no question, and there seems little hope of success for any Thelemic group until this force is understood and dealt with. It is often forgotten that Nuit is the goddess who teaches discrimination, and this virtue is a most necessary one in working with *Liber AL* and its Qaballa."

A small inheritance came along and I was able to purchase a thurible and real incense, and other ritual equipment, together with the Rider Waite Tarot and Dion Fortune's *Mystical Qabalah*, and both volumes of Gareth Knight's *Qabalistic Symbolism*. I also made a double-cube altar which I still use to this day.

I went to an art shop and bought everything I needed for oil painting; I was doing still life compositions and attempting to express the reality I was beginning to see as a result of my occult work. All sorts of everyday things were suddenly alive with deeper significance. Cups and plates, stairs and doorways, numbers, colours, shapes, even the words I thought and spoke; I learned to recognise people's astrological characteristics, and saw those qualities in the Sephirotic attributions, tracing their stories on the Paths of the Tarot. The contents of my mind were being rearranged and I was finding harmony everywhere and I was loving every moment of it. It was like finding a huge orchestra waking up and slowly tuning its instruments to the frequency of the English Qaballa. The group meetings were inspiring and reassuring, for I had no other friends.

The *Book of the Law* seemed to have some business to conduct with me personally, so I dedicated myself to the understanding of what that meant. I was more mystically inclined than interested in conjurations, more interested in answering the questions that seethed and burned in heart and mind than evoking spirits, and I spent much time in contemplative meditation. I studied the phrase "Do what Thou wilt shall be the whole of the Law" and pulled it to bits word by word and letter by letter, hunting for the true meanings of 'Thou' and 'Law' and 'whole' and 'be' within my own psyche. It seemed to me that "Love is the Law, Love under Will" was an affirming reply to the first statement, and together they presented a discipline of personal integrity as strict as any spiritually aspirant code of behaviour. Every act and deed had to be a conscious expression of Love. I referred everything back to the Lexicon of the *Book of the Law*, developing a very personal and intuitive technique, and discovering deep resonances of significant meanings and relationships in corresponding words that seemed quite simple, such as SUN = 36 = MAN; MOON = 49 = MARY; EARTH = 66 = BABE. When I got stuck I would ask for a sign; usually within 24 hours a number or a phrase or an image would appear in circumstances quite beyond my control but synchronistically in parallel with my study, which I would accept as my answer on the basis that nothing happens in isolation.

I was also assimilating the obvious implications of a qaballa in English. Its existence led me to surmise that an unknown power had overlooked the development of the English language from its earliest beginnings. Furthermore it meant that the extension of the alphabet to 26 letters did not happen by accident, that the spellings of words and rules of grammar were not arrived at by some random process, but that all this had happened by design. This conclusion opened up a proposition of far greater import.

The existence of the English Qaballa proves that *Liber AL*, the *Book of the Law*, is a Holy Book.

I could determine some of the prerequisite characteristics of a Holy Book by referring to earlier examples in other languages. For example, they are all given or dictated under rather mysterious circumstances to a mortal man by an equally mysterious and unearthly entity.

A Holy Book, by definition, must reveal the magical structure of the language in which it is written.

A Holy Book must contain a Mechanism of Creation which demonstrably works on all levels of existence.

A Holy Book must delineate the meaning of life – my life, your life, as you or I experience it.

A Holy Book must have the fundamental answers to the fundamental questions such as: what are we here for and where are we going and who is really in charge?

The *Book of the Law* fulfils all of the above criteria.

This proposition demands a coherent universe, and my little microcosm was striving like a butterfly in metamorphosis to become the mirror of the truth I perceived in that coherence.

Jim at that period was exploring a range of E.Qaballistic correspondences pertaining to ONE=46=WOMAN and NUIT=78=FIRE and BABALON=65=GODDESS, and writing copious quantities of notes as he went along, usually on A4 copy paper.

"Can you type?" he asked me one day, and handed me a page of writing. The first years of the1980's were the early days of home computing, and Jim had a BBC B computer and a dot matrix printer. To cut a long story short, I typed up the notes and saved them under a suitable filename, which I made a note of on the manuscript.

"Can you edit this?" Jim asked me a few months later,

handing me a different page of writing. "It's a bit back to front." I did the best I could, and it must have been adequate, for Jim soon asked me again to sort out some notes for him, and in this way I became his secretary. Before long there were a dozen or more files, of varying length and subject matter, so I made an index list file in which I included a short precis of each files' contents; then the PC revolution happened, and I transferred my burgeoning archive to an IBM hard drive and the word processing software of the day. The floppy disks were smaller, the print quality was better, and it was fairly easy to manage a cross-referenced directory of Jim's work. In four or five years I had an index of 17 folder headings such as 'GODDESS' and 'TWOTREES' and 'HORUS' with file-lists stored in each, and a total file list; and I had a temporary folder where I would save work in progress. I was quite certain that this work had to be done and that I was the one to do it; and nobody made any objection.

Inspired Sanguinary Encounter

It was an evening like many others, to begin with at least; group members gathered in the front room with its bookcases and dark red wallpaper and easy spring-loaded rocking chairs, the empty grandfather clock forever silent by the window, and on the other side of the room the plaster statue of the Goddess, ivory coloured and gracefully touching her naked thigh, standing on top of the big Leak speaker in the corner.

Our Chief, Brother Leo, whom we all know as Jim, is there of course, reclining easily on one elbow in front of the fire, and Sister Thelema looking like the Empress with her cascading blonde hair is sitting close by. Brother Thoth, his face pale and eager behind his outsized pipe and black-rimmed glasses, is there; Brother Hersechel is there, enthroned and jovial as always, blue eyes a-twinkle, and Brother Pan too with his unruly hair and mirthful smile, and the conversation is flying around the number 42 and the words in the *Book of the Law* that have that value. The English Qaballa is about six years old, and I am a Neophyte of two years or so, and I sit in the corner saying almost nothing but listening with all my being to the discussion, which swirls in operatic grandeur, peeling away layer after layer of obscurity and falsification as the E.Q. is liable to do, restoring broken or damaged links in a drama older than history and laying it out for us all new and fresh like a bowlful of dewy roses. It was a discussion that had a profound and irreversible effect on me, such that I will never forget it. This is how it happened...

42 is the value of BLOOD and the *Book of the Law* says unequivocally in verse 24 of the third Chapter that menstrual blood is the best. "The best blood is of the moon, monthly." This is old magickal and alchemical tradition, menstrual blood having the distinction of being the 'Universal Solvent' and possessing all sorts of other properties mentioned in veiled and allegorical terms in the old books of lore. In other areas and ages of society menstruation is deep taboo, and customs of isolating a woman while she is menstruating are very common. Obviously there is something very special going on in the female physiology at this time of the month, and it is as AL suggests an intimate Mystery of the Moon. The exercise is to arrive at an understanding of this mystery by way of other words adding to 42.

CROSS is 42. We in the group are all Christian by upbringing and so the association with BLOOD is easy. Blood was shed upon the Cross, and E.Q. says there is a parallel with the shedding of menstrual blood. The womb lining is sacrificed which causes the effusion, but more importantly the womb is renewed and made ready once more to nurture life.

Sister Thelema and I nod and murmur our agreement, indeed we do feel renewed after our period is over, and Sister Thelema adds the observation that in a close community women tend to menstruate together. The word 'redeemed' pops up. The blood on the Cross redeems mankind, and the blood of the Moon, monthly, redeems Woman. It is magickally significant because it is a vehicle for the potential creation of life.

Thoth remarks that 'Adam' means 'red earth' and Pan adds something about *Liber AL*'s five pointed Star with its central red circle. We wander off a bit, and Leo reminds us that STAR is another 42.

We talk about timing. It seems clear that a woman ought to bleed when the Moon is in Scorpio, which we know is a time when everything dies. It corresponds with Autumn, and the time of maximum fertility is the opposite end of the Zodiac, Taurus, springtime. A hush falls as we remember that the festival of Easter is timed to the first full moon after the Spring Equinox which means that it is synchronised with Moon in Scorpio. Then somebody says "KISS adds up to 42 as well," so we can see the necessity of the Gethsemane ritual and why we use the X cross to represent a kiss. The words in AL I:53 about the regeneration of the world "unto whom I send this kiss" slide into place in confirmation of our analysis.

We are cooking with gas tonight. The atmosphere in the room is alive with energy as the vortex of shared enthusiasm gets into gear, spinning between the assembled minds, shiny-eyed like children on Christmas morning opening rare and splendid gifts from the gods themselves.

The red circle seems to refer to the periods of bleeding which don't happen because of conception having occurred, between 40 and 45 days' worth of blood turned over as it were to the making of a child. The Star in question has association with the colour red through the number 5 and the 5th Sephiroth Geburah whose mundane Chakra is Mars the red planet. All these reds come from the metal iron, which the scientists say is at the core of all the planets in the Solar system, and which we know is a significant constituent of blood, being present in haemoglobin which carries molecules of oxygen around. The pentagram is a symbol of Adam who was made from red earth. It's all about life and the vessel which bears life. RED has the same value as A STAR, 43, and we are all stars, *Liber AL* tells us that in the third verse, "Every man and every woman is a Star." MARS = 39 = YOU, the energy which is you, and me, is this same symbol of the red circle within the five-pointed star.

Iron captures our attention for a while. Pan works out its value, 56, and Leo (who is a knowledgeable alchemist) tells us that its atomic weight is also 56, which seems a pleasant symmetry. We talk about magnets and maritime compasses and the earth's magnetic field. Iron is definitely a magickal metal. The number 56 brings us back to the Goddess, Her Name ISIS having the same value, and the five days of light she won from the Moon God Thoth to recreate the body of Osiris now make sense as the length of the menstrual period. It dawns on us that although the name of Isis is absent from the *Book of the Law*, the ibis-headed Thoth is in there in his Greek form, Tahuti. Which is a Name whose value is 93.

We laugh, but nervously. We are being led by an unseen hand, gentle but insistent. We know a little bit about Scorpio's dark secrets, and we circle round again. *How many Scorpios does it take to change a lightbulb? – none, they prefer to sit in the dark.* Hersechel, with his capacious memory for astrological charts, recalls a few people born under this Sign and affirms their curious delight in concealment, and habitual dropping of the *bon mot* that will assassinate a conversation in a moment, the sting in the tail that as often as not leads to their own downfall.

Leo talks about Horary astrology which is the divinatory branch of the ancient art, describing how the moon in Scorpio is the spanner in the astrologer's work which renders the chart useless. Horary interpretation is largely concerned with the moon's aspects as she moves through the Sign in which she is found in the chart, but if she is in Scorpio then nothing can be predicted and the chart should be discarded immediately. The dangerous period is actually between 15 degrees Libra and 15 degrees Scorpio, which brings us to another interesting diversion, of the tradition of the 'thirteenth Sign' and Ophiucchus the Serpent-bearer whose constellation spans that part of the sky between Scorpio and Sagittarius. We dip back into the story of Isis as well for a moment, scorpions having a part to play in the wanderings of the Goddess and again in the birth and early life of her magickal Child, Horus.

Like the Wise Men of old, however, the Star 42 beckons us to follow all the way back to the Nativity, where the Virgin's Mona Lisa smile greets us with her number – which is of course 93. The most unpredictable event of all is the Virgin Birth.

Now we are really getting somewhere. The significance of the Moon is borne out by its value 49 – KEY. We debate the phases of the Moon in relation to the menstrual cycle and quickly agree that the full moon represents maximum fertility, and the new moon or rather the dark of the moon represents the bleed, and the Zodiacal correspondences are accordingly Taurus and Scorpio. 93 is beginning to loom rather large in all this, and we are using the number as shorthand for "the Moon being in Scorpio" which as we have discovered is not simply a bad time for horary astrology but also a time when the impossible event does actually occur.

Not only does VIRGIN add to 93, but MOTHER does as well, and NATURE also is 93. This makes sense, Nature is the Great Mother, and She is ever Virgin. Then somebody points out that the average distance between Planet Earth and the Sun is another 93, in millions of miles, and we throw up our hands and laugh out loud. It would have to be that far, what they call the Goldilocks zone where it's not too hot nor too cold but just right for the most unlikely event in the history of the Universe, the appearance, survival, and development of conscious self-aware Life.

We calm down and recap to see where we have got to, because the journey is not quite complete. We have been talking for hours, the sky will be getting light soon with the first glow of dawn, and the energy we are sharing drives us onwards and we are hardly aware of anything else. We have got to the harbour, but we have not yet dropped anchor.

Scorpio, when the Moon is in Scorpio, 93, is the time when interesting things happen. The unexpected becomes normal, the impossible becomes necessary under the aegis of 93.

And what about the Crucifixion? – at what other time could one crucify a God, if not in Scorpio? – and when would a dead body be able to rise and roll back the stone, to be met first by a Moon Priestess?

The point is that the death is only an apparent death, a sacrifice which ensures the preservation of life, just as the fallen leaves of Autumn enrich the soil for new seed germination, just as the womb is renewed for new life, (NEW=42=STAR, BLOOD, CROSS), it is all the same story. Centuries of misinterpretation and fragmentation disappear like morning mist.

This is the keystone of the Qaballistic bridge we have built between the past and the present, between myth and reality, the allegory which has been hidden in plain sight for so long – that the Phoenix rises once more from its ashes, that the Green Man is recreated every year, that there is the Resurrection, that life is eternal and death is just a change of scenery. These are realities as plain as the nose on your face, overlooked and taken for granted most often because familiarity breeds negligence before contempt. In Scorpio one could almost certainly turn lead into gold, providing always that one fully and sincerely expects to fail. We begin to consider 93 as a possible matrix for ritual, all the more keenly when Brother Thoth says that another 93 in the *Book of the Law* is the phrase THAT HOUR, indicating a precisely timed rite. The current ephemeris, never very far away, is consulted and we find that we are within a couple of days of the next 93. With this we realise that tomorrow is becoming yesterday and we really should go home and get some rest.

I spend the rest of the night and morning tucked away in my bedsit flat, writing and meditating and generally messing about with the numbers and the words. My mind has been taken apart and put back together again in what feels like a sublime orgy of initiation. I am a young woman, I bleed, I was brought up Christianwise, and all this is right where I live, this revelation is a revolution in my innermost female self and it all feels right and true, nothing is strained or fudged or left out. All the pieces fit. I go to the bathroom, and find that my period has come, a bit early, but English Qaballa does do synchronicity in really good style... a drop of blood has landed on the back of my hand. I stare at it, transfixed, and feel nameless emotion rising and rising in me. Surging mental ecstasy, my heart throbbing with joy and wonder, I stare at this drop of blood standing there proud and gleaming like a ruby, like a star. The top of my head has vanished and my consciousness is filling with boundless golden light streaming from above, stabbing gently into my heart and overflowing and suffusing my entire being in warm perfect certainty. For I am looking at a living symbol of miracle, the promised kiss, the body of the Word made Flesh, the confirmation of every dawn's heart-searching flame, the actual real tangible demonstrable possibility of a new life.

It was the difference between assimilating the information of the previous night so that I could say with confidence "I know this" (meaning "I think I know this") and the internal realisation of the facts laid before me so that the intellectual knowledge became spiritual gnosis, part of my womanhood. The new life was mine, and I have never looked back. In those moments of ecstatic vision my female soul sprang free of all restraint engendered by social attitudes built on who knows how many thousands of years' worth of fear. Not that I had that much internal conflict about bleeding, my mother with several Suffragists in her lineage simply told me I had become a woman, but the superstitions are old and powerful and form an effective veil that I'd not noticed until it was obliterated. There was no longer any compromise with the simple faith of my childhood, no argument or doubt of this truth, this reflection of macrocosmic reality in my bit of microcosm. I had come to a state of certainty.

Years later I wrote a poem which goes some way towards an inadequate descriptive expression of this experience.

THE RUBY STAR REVISITED

I was getting dressed
When I first met you.
You fell warm and soft
On the back of my hand
Like an old dream
Freshly remembered…

(Though you brought me my womanhood
Many years before, I did not know you
Did not expect your existence behind your shroud of
centuries.)

You stretched
My female soul to the universe
Strange filaments leaped
From every vein to every star
You sparked the holy flame
To burn inside my mind, my womb –
Glory to bear this glory! –
I stand united with the earth mother
And silently behold the sacrificed son.

(What awesome joyous certainty
This secret temple, secret inner self,
Engorged and blazing with the shape of blood slow and red
on white skin.)

And you
Revealed to me that you had purified

My shameless body
Returned to me my woman's pride
Numbed and scarred no more
But smooth and crystal clear, and strong –
Transcending all the ages! –
Saying 'this will be your sign for ever,
This is certainty that you will always know.'

(Yes I welcome the burning ache
The redeeming star, my blood on the cross
The mysteries of creation in the moment of death for life.)

And when the day comes
I dress like a queen
The proud diadem
On the back of my hand
Like an old dream
Freshly remembered….

Improbable Stellar Arrangement

WITH MY SPIRITUALITY realigned and redeemed from ancestral indoctrinations I went on with my daily Pentagrams and Middle Pillar meditations, and one day about eighteen months later I found myself in a place where I knew that God is Love. My notion of God was based on my understanding of the words in the first chapter of *Liber AL*, "I am divided for love's sake, for the chance of union... this is the Creation of the World," and I saw a rather abstract and androgynous omnipresence. Now, gloriously, I saw that its power was Love, and while I felt love in my heart I was feeling that Presence. The radiance of it spread through me till it overwhelmed me utterly and I was filled with vibrant beautiful loving ecstasy. I knew that all Creation was for love's sake, that the force which holds atoms together and keeps planets in orbit is the Eternal and infinite Love that is the expression of the One Supreme Deity. I stood in the Presence of That, and I knew that it was true. Moreover, as I came back to myself, I knew that I had been granted a verifiable Vision such as others had seen before me, and which would always remain locked in my being, impossible to remove, a certainty beyond doubt. Now I could say, "I know this, because I've been there and seen it." I was walking on air, and very impressed with myself; the glow of ecstasy was pervading my whole being and I felt I must be lit up like a Christmas Tree.

I described my vision to Jim and he smiled and said "Ah! there speaks someone who thinks they've seen the Truth," and indeed I felt that I had arrived and was now properly enlightened. Of course I had only made the first step, and the radiant confidence that oozed from every pore imperceptibly faded as I got used to it over the ensuing months. Eventually all the light went out and all I had left was the certainty itself, like a single tiny star in the deep blackness of the desert night, and I was lost, bereft and orphaned in that terrible darkness. I had horrible nightmares in which I would be trapped in a collapsing building, and I would wake in a cold sweat to the conviction that I was about to die, and lie there in the silence, heart pounding, gripped with fear and dread.

These panic attacks happened in waves lasting a month or more for three or four years, until I gave up one night and said "OK, I'm ready, go on, kill me" and completely accepted the immediate inevitability of death, welcoming that which I had been resisting. I was released from my fear to such an extent that after a while I actually missed it, and reinvoked it deliberately to see if I could handle it, but that mind-numbing panic never returned except briefly, quite reasonably and sensibly under conditions that seemed genuinely life-threatening, when the instant full alertness of the adrenaline shot was very useful.

I had read widely enough to suspect that I was experiencing the condition known as the Dark Night of the Soul, but there seemed no remedy for me, no light in my darkened mind as Reason and Emotion conflicted and shuttled me to and fro, shaking me to pieces. All that I thought I knew to be reliably solid and true was turning to mush. I felt isolated from everything and balanced on a knife edge above a pit of madness; I painted some awful pictures in colours of decay, and strove to appear normal while inside I was disintegrating in despair as every analysis was proved false, every conclusion and interpretation erroneous. It went on for about eight years, signified in my astrology with a Sun conjunct Mercury, opposite Saturn, and square Neptune, during which interval many other more interesting and entertaining events occurred.

It was a wonderfully spontaneous period. One never knew what to expect when calling at Jim's; sometimes there would be guests from America, Europe, or nearer to home, bringing new occult flavours; or someone might bring a rare aphrodisiac or liqueur, or a curious herb, and occasionally a few grams of cannabis. Volunteers stepped up to test the latest substance, and later make their reports; thus the group had a variety of ordeal poisons at their disposal. One candidate blindfolded for initiation was properly surprised by a spot of cinnamon oil on the forehead; it produces a short-lived but intense burning sensation within a minute or so which made him suck in his breath in a most satisfactory fashion.

On one occasion an out-of-town occultist and his wife were visiting on a beneficial planetary aspect, and joined in the celebratory garden feast with enthusiasm. They were eager to impress, but it was observed that the joints gathered up at their end and they were tardy in passing along. Accordingly, some of the strongest weed we had was rolled up and passed down. A short while later the male half of the sketch got up and ventured back towards the house, and when he did not reappear his wife went to check on his whereabouts. When she came back to the group, relaxing in post-prandial somnolence, we asked where her man had got to. With the sweetest of smiles she loyally confided that "he was in a trance", and when curiosity enticed us indoors to make sure, the gentleman was indeed discovered in a kneeling position, eyes closed and head bowed, and not disposed to communicate with earthly beings such as ourselves. He was unhappy but all right, so we left him to it, and he eventually emerged pale and unsteady, but strong enough to graciously acknowledge the sprinkle of ironic applause.

The group's researches into the Sun-Venus aspect were reaching the point where another major ritual was obviously the next step, to put into practice some of the theories that had formed since the 1981 ritual. We would make sure this time that it was rightly performed, and it seemed only fair to invite Jake and his group to join us. The Ephemeris came out, and after a brief investigation our attention was drawn to a Sun conjunct Venus occurring a week before the midsummer solstice of 1984. The aspect seemed relatively free from affliction. The Moon was not well placed in Capricorn but that did not give us any concern, the other malefic planets were too far away in degrees to matter, and I do not believe we took any notice of the applying trine to Pluto where he stood on the cusp of Scorpio. Taken all in all it seemed an opportunity that we should not miss, and we began to work on the possibilities.

Having agreed the date, the question was where to perform this Supreme Ritual, and considering that we were looking at a midsummer meet the best plan seemed to be to go up to the woods and make it a somewhat witchy celebration, with a properly built fire using branches from the nine traditionally sacred trees. Brother Pan went to check the integrity of the Circle, and reported it to be in good condition. He and Brother Hersechel undertook the task of making the torches in the usual way with bundles of cloth soaked in wax and secured on poles. With that proposition being agreeable to all, we turned to the feasting arrangements, for it was plain that we could not do a woodland rite and then drive home for the feast; therefore we would take our feast with us. The steak would cook over charcoal at the fire's edge, we could roast potatoes in tin foil, and take whole roast chicken to eat cold. The cream cakes came in the baker's trays, making for easy portage. We would take tents and sleeping bags, and make caches of water and tinned food in advance. Moreover, with the aspect forming late on the Friday night, we would extend the ritual to fill two nights and three days with feasting and suitable periods for recovering, beginning with the symbolic stripping of identities and powers from the ritualists by the supreme power of the Sun-Venus conjunction, followed by a period of chaos (a word that had lately gained popularity following the publication of Peter J. Carroll's books *Liber Null* and *Psychonaut*, and certain advances in particle physics), and culminating in the re-appointing and blessing of the planetary officers by the Priest and Priestess.

Jake was keen as mustard, promising at least half a dozen members of his group with their own tents, a minibus, and whatever else he could gather up. We made our preparations, individually in private, and together in the woods, carrying non-perishable supplies and collecting the different types of firewood including some big oak roots for their charcoal which has long-lasting heat and imparts a delicious flavour, and concealing all in the bracken and brambles to the North and East of the Circle.

Summer '84. Clockwise from top left:
Cath Thompson, Jake Stratton-Kent, Carol Smith, James Lees.

Jim had recently acquired a video camera, and we thought we might film parts of the ritual. It was a VHS camcorder and quite portable, with a separate battery pack in a leather case with a shoulder strap, which ran for several hours on a full charge, and the equipment lent a slight professionalism to the appearance of its bearer. Somebody joked that we could excuse our presence in the woods with a tale of film-making, a remark soon forgotten but which came back to seal our fate later on, propelling us for a brief space onto the front pages of the national press.

When Jake arrived with his people the group was sixteen strong. There were one or two new faces present as we greeted each other, and then took them to see what we had assembled for the feasts: eight cold roast chickens, eight pounds of best steak, cartons of fruit and salad, and milk, two dozen hardboiled eggs, three or four sliced loaves of white bread and a couple of brown wholemeal, a pound or two of butter and a large array of cream cakes; the camcorder and its battery pack; and of course a full selection of robes, incense, planetary weapons and assorted ritual equipment. This was what had to be taken up to the camp site along with their own belongings. Already in place, we explained, was enough champagne and wine to entertain a small fleet, gallons of water, tea, coffee, sugar, tinned food, and all the frying pans, saucepans, knives, forks, tin openers and corkscrews, spoons, mugs, paper plates and plastic cups (more practical than china and glass), and aspirin and toilet rolls that we were likely to need.

It was some distance to walk from the car-park and uphill through the wood to the Circle. We did not want to leave a line of vehicles parked by the roadside entrance to the woods, so there was a certain amount of to-and-fro driving through the adjacent village, and we did not pass unnoticed into the woods. We went in bands of three or four, all carrying something, our members showing the others by different routes and most of us making a good deal of noise. A curious passer-by was given the film-crew story, but unfortunately he was a local farmer with sheep in a field on the far side of the wood and he remained unconvinced.

Of course we had no knowledge of this. As the warm summer night drew in the atmosphere seemed perfect, with a faint breeze whispering of friendly woodland spirits gathered in the dusk, and we happily pitched our tents and collected wood for a camp fire. The Circle had been swept and the Balefire was already prepared, carefully constructed and not too big, for it was summertime and dry, and the fire-damage of eight summers ago was still a visible caution. Tea was brewed and we got ourselves settled in around the perimeter of the Circle, our ritual paraphernalia to hand, and the first feast laid out; seven torches had suitable holes made for their poles and stood ready.

Then the stillness of the woods took us and we hushed ourselves, our preparations complete under the canopy of birch and beech with the darkling blue sky above, and then, with a fond glance at the food, we put on our robes.

The Circle was drawn and the first words rang out in the dusk.

"What is the Hour?"

"When Time has no Power!" we replied.

"What is the Place?"

"At the limits of Space!"

"What God do we wake?" and so forth, establishing the purpose of the Ritual; meanwhile the Thurible was prepared for the Purification of the Circle. The Consecration with Water followed, and we all entered the Circle from the North and spread out around the circumference. Then the Balefire was lit, and the torches dipped to the flames; the Lesser Banishing Pentagram Rite was performed, and after that the Bornless Rite, and all members added their visualisations to aid the Officer's work. Invocations of the Sun and Venus followed, and then each member laid his weapons and symbols of office at the feet of the Venus Priestess, and disrobed, nakedness symbolising the total lack of identification with any image or personality. Finally the Priest and Priestess disrobed, and we all sat down to drink the first of many toasts. Muffled yelps and expressions of discomfort were heard from those who had never done this before; the more experienced of us gathered heaps of dead leaves to serve as cushions. More toasts were drunk, and the frying pans were brought into action for the steak. Joints were lit and passed, and more toasts drunk.

"Here's to Chaos!"

"Io Pan!"

"Io Chaos!"

"– how's the steak doing?"

"More wine!"

"I'll drink to that!"

"Hooray for chaos!"

"Chaos!"

"Food!"

"A toast to the cooks!"

– and it was time for the Feast, and more wine, and then the cream cakes came round, and we toasted the baker too. To burn off the stupefaction of the wine we got up and began to dance around the fire, twirling and weaving and falling over, staggering upright and pulling each other relentlessly on, with shouts of "Chaos!" and breathless laughter. The High Priestess led us out of the Circle and into the old Chain-Dance through the trees, calling us on, skipping and dancing over and around stumps and fallen branches, and we followed along "as falcons gray, and black tom-cats, and swift greyhounds", hunting behind as she led us home, and the Master's baying voice at the back hurrying us forward.

Suddenly there was another voice, strange and hostile. Suddenly there came the flash of an electric torch stark and white in the darkness near the bale-fire. Suddenly everything crashed, and I had a split second in the Middle Ages facing a mob armed with pitchforks and hayrakes. We shrank together in shock, immediately aware of our acute vulnerability, recognising the distinctive police helmets and uniforms in the firelight. There was nothing to be done but return to the Circle.

Unfortunate Arboreal Interruption

Two genuine 20th century policemen and a police woman beckoned us back to the campsite. We did the sensible thing and went, our Chief suggesting quietly and calmly that all we could hope for was a little basic humanity in return for our unquestioning cooperation. We dressed in stunned silence, some of us gave our names and addresses, one or two stood and wept and were comforted by those of us who felt a bit stronger. We were asked to wait while transport was arranged to take us back into town.

As we waited we began to revive and recover enough to take stock and start to make the best of what looked to be an appallingly bad situation. Fifteen years of peaceful anonymity had been shattered; our Circle was desecrated, our ritual had been most rudely interrupted. We had not actually been arrested, but we could only hope that someone had managed to dispose of the remaining cannabis. But, having invoked Chaos with such enthusiasm, we could not help but recognise the irony of the situation, and we wondered what our three officers of the Law thought about it, especially as there had been an outcry in the media recently against the prevalence of Freemasonry in the police force.

We gathered up our bedraggled spirits and sat round the fire waiting for the transport and singing, "Green Grow the Rushes-Oh!" Some time passed before the arrival of a ten-seater minibus was announced, and when we fetched up at the roadside we saw what looked like every police car in the county for an escort.

"They've all come to see what's happening, we're a star attraction!"

"Do you think they want autographs?"

"Can we all get in this minibus?"

"Of course we can, just squash up a bit."

"Hey, this must be over the limit!"

"This is illegal, you're not supposed to have sixteen people in a thing this size!"

"We'll be arrested on the way back."

"No we won't, the police are all here already!"

One or two of the men were observed to have distinct grins as the arrangements were made and the convoy got under way. We were beginning to have an effect on our new friends. We bantered and giggled all the way into town and the cells in the police station, where the ladies were given a separate room and a policewoman to take details of names and addresses. Sixteen sets of forms were filled in, and we settled to the vigil of waiting for whatever was next. The ritual was continuing, even if not exactly as planned.

In the pre-dawn light four of us were allowed back up to the woods under supervision to collect everything up and tidy the site. At this point the cannabis was discovered, an amount just under a quarter of an ounce, in those days worth no more than £20 at the most. So everything had to remain in situ until they were sure there was nothing else; we were officially charged with possession, provided with mattresses to sit on, and locked in for the remainder of the night. Things were looking a bit bleak, and we priestesses resolved to be sensible and got what rest we could.

Eventually there came the sounds of the outside world waking up to Saturday, and the thought of coffee became prominent. Sister Maat and I poked our arms through the bars as if we were in the Wild West, and made noise until a desk sergeant came along the corridor. He was sorry, but would we please shut up, because they had nothing for our refreshment – nor his – until the local café opened. We cooed sympathetically, and asked after our menfolk. We would be allowed to see them shortly.

In a while we were escorted to the larger cell where the men were incarcerated and briefly discussed the situation. We agreed unanimously that there would not be a scapegoat, that we would all take responsibility for something which had been brought for all of us, and stand together to face whatever the penalty would be. We were given platefuls of toast and mugs of tea when the day shift began, and treated more as special guests than as criminals by the new shift of police officers, who had missed all the fun and did not want to let their disappointment show.

Now we were waiting for two officers of the local Drug Squad and a sniffer dog who had been called in to hunt through our belongings for more illegal substances. The team arrived after some delay to much anticipation and excitement from the local force, who were expecting a professional display of canine training. The unlucky animal's olfactory senses were functioning according to their design parameters, and when presented with our campsite the dog headed straight for the cold roast chicken and thereafter showed no interest whatsoever in tracking down anything else.

By now we were in fairly high spirits again. A deputation had been sent to collect the van owned by Jake's contingent which contained all our equipment, and what was left of our food and wine. Our Chief gave a careful interview and statement, and then we were called out in pairs to be fingerprinted and photographed and finally released. We larked about like children, grumbling about our inky fingers and chattering away to any officer of the Law who would listen, and waving farewell, blowing kisses, saluting and bowing as we left, asking if we could come back next year, and thanking them all profusely.

Throughout the afternoon a steady trickle of exhausted but determined people might have been observed wearily making their way from the police station to the nearest 'safe house' where they brewed copious amounts of strong coffee, and collapsed in shattered silent heaps in a room which in happier times had been used as a temple. Here we stayed, slowly regrouping and recovering our equilibrium.

As we shared our impressions and reactions we agreed we had all been surprised to learn that there were no facilities for making tea or coffee in the police station. It seemed a shame, especially as they had treated us so respectfully, and so we took up a collection and Sister Maat and I went into the town and bought an electric tea and coffee making machine which we presented to the staff of the police station "from the O∴A∴A∴ with thanks for your kindness".

Finally we held our second feast, and then slept where we lay. The next day we celebrated the final ritual more or less as we had planned, and then relaxed with a well-earned and much needed afternoon of sunbathing, in the hottest temperatures of the year.

Headline collage by Cath Thompson.

    The story hit our local papers the following week, and then made the nationals. It was the silly season, and the story sold the town's newspapers for a couple of months afterwards, but Fleet Street ignored us until we appeared in court in September, where we behaved angelically and were fined a total of £2000.

A dozen or so professional tabloid reporters and photographers had arrived in town for the trial, looking for sex, drugs, devil-worship, and secret midnight orgies, and Jim invited me to come and join the throng in his front room. It was an intense experience; Jim handed me a generous double brandy as I entered, saying, "You might need this." Within a short space of time the glass was empty and I was fired up and wide awake, the alcohol fuelling my nervous energy without any inebriated befuddlement. Some other group members were also present, equally switched on and knowing roughly what was coming.

The reporters were poised and ready to start, when Jim asked them flatly what sort of story their editors had told them to get, and then, having taken the wind out of their sails and shot one or two masts away into the bargain, he started to tell them a story. He showed them an occult reality which captured their attention to such an extent that one of them put his notebook down and simply listened, while some others just forgot to write after a while.

Jim wove a spell around them all; he told them about astrological timing and the Hermetic principles of magic and the English Qaballa, and he told them that we had been attempting to avert a national disaster, and finally he told them that they would not be able to print a word of it. The Moon was in Scorpio again, and sure enough She interfered with the plans and intentions of our guests, spiking the stories in the manner of the creature of Her Sign, so that only the basic reports of the court proceedings were printed, and no further interviews were ever sought with anyone. One of the photographers took a few group shots of Jim, Carol, Jake, and me; I happened to meet him again a couple of months later and he gave me a nice 8"x10" print.

Some time after the furore had died down an acquaintance of ours was in a builder's merchant being served by a man who had known Jim simply as a good customer who bought plumbing and electrical supplies – before the story hit the front page of the town's weekly newspaper.

"Funny goings on, eh?" said the shopkeeper. "Tell you the truth, I don't know that I could look him in the face again, not after all this."

Our friend gave him a long hard stare.

"You ought to be careful of what you say," he said, "you never know who you're talking to!" And with a wink, he departed.

We were, of course, written and talked about locally as 'witches' for several weeks, but there was no unpleasantness inflicted upon us, and it seemed we might return to our former obscurity, except that the Supreme Ritual was already causing deep and permanent changes both individually and collectively.

We had no Temple at all, and in any case we were all nursing our burned fingers and not over-keen to don robes and breathe incense again. The group fractured within eighteen months, and a few members resigned. Some left the area completely and were hardly heard from again. At the same time members of Jake's group migrated in our direction, and we managed to find a temporary space for a Temple to conduct one or two more initiations, but the next couple of years were a very difficult and disturbed period.

Sometime in the following autumn Jim asked me if I'd ever tried engraving, and when I replied in the negative but with enthusiasm for the idea, he gave me a flat disk of white marble and an electric engraving tool and bade me go to it. I filled my bedsit with white dust and destroyed the engraver by wrapping it in a towel when it got too hot to hold, but it was a good piece of work. Jim was pleased with it, and later filled out the design with gold leaf. He was quite unconcerned about the melted engraver when I somewhat ruefully handed it back to him. He had known artists in the beatnik days of Manchester in the 1950's, and understood how easily the Muse overcomes common sense; he sat me down and gave me Crowley's essay on "Energized Enthusiasm" to read, which of course stoked my fire even more.

One of our new members from the south-west was the late Trevor Langford, Brother Daedalus, a cheerful Aries with a disarmingly boyish grin and laughing eyes under an untidy mop of brown hair, and a leaping abundance of enthusiasm. One day, having seen the marble Pantacle and the remains of the engraver, he gave me an industrial model which was made of tougher stuff; I still have it and employ it occasionally.

Trevor was a computer programmer of exceptional talent and he could make the BBC computer stand up and eat out of his hand. Requiring only a supply of cherry brandy, Trevor wrote the first English Qaballa software, which would "crunch the numbers" as he put it, and calculate word, phrase, and sentence values, compile wordlists, and perform letter and word frequency analyses. Once I had the text of *Liber AL* accurately typed in, Trevor went to work and soon produced statistical analyses of the three chapters which showed that the letter "S" is the most frequently used in *Liber AL* by an appreciable margin. Then I typed in the rest of the Class A documents and some of Crowley's poetry, and one or two other pieces of English

Literature of comparable length and it was plain to see from the letter frequency that *Liber AL*'s author was less and less involved with the other texts called Class A as Crowley's own identity came to the fore and the normal pattern of letter frequency emerged in which the letter "E" is by far the most common.

Jim had some astrological software which Trevor hacked into and turned into an astrology program that I have never seen equalled since. It could produce natal, progressed, and converse charts and aspects across them all, plus transits, with interpretations from Alan Leo and Reinhold Ebertin (I think it was a quarter of a million words that I typed in), and print them all out, a year's worth at a time. Trevor even wrote a synastry program, so that we could account for the characteristics of relationships both within the group and beyond. There were no published synastry interpretations that we knew of so Jim invoked his Muse and wrote a complete set in one sitting, and I typed them up too. Everything was stored on floppy disks and Trevor's astrology program ran across four of them in two disk drives at once; someone would have to watch for the monitor to display instructions to swap disks, and eventually there would be printout, slowly spooling from the dot-matrix machine to the floor in a continuous zig-zag stream, which had to be separated into sheets by tearing along the perforated edges. I was not an accurate typist and there were numerous errors, but nobody seemed to mind.

Then Trevor wrote a program which calculated the time of every planet's conjunction with the Part of Fortune, every day for a month, and printed the data in neat lists. Fortuna has an orb of just eight minutes, which makes for some very precisely timed rituals with planetary alignments;

its position is found with a deceptively simple formula of Ascendant plus Moon minus Sun, which our E. Qaballistic studies had revealed as the astrological qualitative synthesis of the Holy Grail. To explain briefly, the Sun is the light of individuality, astrologically speaking, while the Moon is the personality and the Ascendant signifies the characteristics of the ego. Without the reflection of the Light from the Sun, the ego/personality combination is an empty negativity, symbolised by the supreme harmony of the Cross in the Circle. At the moment of conjunction the Part of Fortune mediates the planetary force from the celestial macrocosm to the microcosm of the ritual; its function is essentially to give spiritual wealth.

For which there is no substitute!

This hypothesis opened the door to a new field of experimentation which we could begin to discover almost immediately. All we needed was an agreed ritual structure that we could all use, for it would have to be individual work since we still lacked a Temple, and we had to be able to compare our results. We were refining our Stellar Magick by our researches, defining principles taken from horary and natal astrology, finding out the hard way what were the best and worst configurations. Our basic premise was that the characteristics of any moment in time are defined by the astrological factors in force at that moment, and anything begun then will have that astrology imprinted upon it in the way that a nativity or birth chart imprints the life of the individual.

In a single afternoon Jim wrote a set of planetary invocations suitable for new initiates and old hands alike. (In later years these rituals were made available to all via the internet, and in 2017 they were included in my second book, *A Handbook of Stellar Magick* published by Hadean Press, with guidelines developed from our own experience.) Their construction is based on Golden Dawn tradition and they are easy and quick to perform, and capable of producing quite startling results. We turned our attention to the possibilities of magickal operations aligned with moments in time, and agreed that the most suitable work for those conditions was the creation of talismans.

We had handmade paper, and we had beeswax, and some of us had already made talismans with these materials. Small rough castings of tin were possible due to the low melting point of the metal, but Trevor had a job at a local foundry, and Jim had once been an analytical chemist in a metallurgical laboratory attached to a bronze foundry, and together with Brother Pan they came up with a plan for forging our own copper and bronze talismans.

Synchronised Metallurgical Adventure

Trevor was in a position to acquire a quantity of the special sand used for making molds for bronze casting. The different alloys of tin and copper was one of Jim's areas of expertise, and he could accurately judge the percentages of the different metals in a bronze casting from the colour and the shine of it, or from the texture of the top surface of the casting, if the piece was still rough and unfinished or "unfettled" on the back.

It seemed only in the natural order of things, therefore, that once the sand appeared, there would soon come an empty oil drum and a number of fire bricks, followed by fire cement, a gas connection and a vacuum cleaner set on "blow", all collected under a purpose built lean-to roof of corrugated iron anchored to an outhouse in the Northeast corner of Jim's garden. Then there was the assembly of a furnace which was designed to generate enough heat to melt copper. A crucible and tongs completed the equipment, and fine grade plaster for me to make the patterns for the molds.

I cast disks and rectangles of the plaster and carved them in bas-relief, making Egyptian deities and a couple of talismans from the Key of Solomon and other designs for various purposes. Biscuit tins were filled with the special sand, and the different patterns pressed in and carefully lifted off again. Molding sand has an adhesive dampness such as makes good sandcastles, but with much smaller grains which allow finer details to be reproduced. A channel is scraped from the edge of the impression for the molten metal to run along, the skill of the pouring being to ensure an even stream which will smoothly fill the mold all at once without stopping anywhere and without air bubbles or overflow. When the casting comes out the extra metal from the channel (called a "sprue") is removed and the piece is fettled up, the wrinkles of the air-cooled surface can be ground smooth, small casting errors filed away, and the whole piece made lovely and shiny with polish.

Making Bronze: Mold Pattern; Bronze Casting; Fettled and Polished Isis Plaque.

Bronze casting is a strange and primal affair with its own curious atmosphere and smells, and it likes to be done in dim light or near dark. Metal working is somehow a mysterious and secretive magic art, as the mythology suggests, and we spent many happy pre-dawn hours heating up our forge. We worked with copper and bronze, and once in a prolonged experiment we made an interesting alloy of the seven planetary metals.

The dawn conjunction of Fortuna with the Moon when that luminary was well aspected by Venus or Jupiter or preferably both was the kind of astrological configuration we preferred for this work. We could see the eastern horizon from where we hovered gnome-like around our darkened forge, its red glow increasing in intensity as the dawn came up, and we made our talismans in the very moment.

We still had no permanent Temple, and scoured the countryside in search of suitable locations. Brother Hersechel found a stone circle that was less than an hour's drive away in the Derbyshire hills, and we tried it with a Sun-Jupiter ritual. It was a pleasant spot with quite a homely atmosphere but it was very windy, and a bit small, we thought. However, the expedition had sparked an interest in stone circles, and there was another really promising set of aspects coming up in early February 1986. It was a multiple conjunction of the Sun, Mercury, Venus, and Jupiter, with a lunar sequence translating light across all of them – a most impressive stellar combination, of which we would dearly like to take advantage.

There were three women and seven men in the group at that time, all well versed in the practice of stellar magic. The group was named The Continuum of the O.·.A.·.A.·.. Each individual was ritually identified with the planet most suited to his character and temperament by its prominence in the natal and progressed chart, and we were all accustomed to the demands of our particular planetary identity. Our three Priestesses took on the three aspects of the Goddess represented by the Moon, Venus and Saturn; in ritual we called each other by our planetary names, and Temple duties and ritual components were presided over by the appropriate planetary officer. Mars was the temple guard, the Sun looked after the element of Fire, the Moon was responsible for Water, Mercury performed the banishing rites, Saturn looked after the timing, and so on. In this way the group became a very potent microcosm or representation of the Solar System.

The best available Stellar Temple in England was obviously the circle at Stonehenge. Jim wrote to the organisation responsible for Stonehenge, English Heritage, who seemed pleased to accept our presence on the given date, and we carefully made our plans.

Two members would drive the two hundred miles down to Glastonbury the day before with a small touring caravan which would be our robing room, with all the necessary robes and ritual equipment on board, and a gas stove on which food and drinks would be prepared. The rest of us would assemble pre-dawn, and as our Stellar Deities in their Mundane Chakras were kissed by Fortuna on her way over the Eastern horizon we would cast a set of talismans using our planetary alloy, and set off, arriving at Stonehenge in good time to meet our advance guard.

In addition to the consecration of our talismans we intended to inaugurate and sign a new Constitution of our Continuum. This document was handwritten on a big sheet of handmade paper; I executed the calligraphy in the legal style known as "engrossing" with all the proper curly flourishes, and Brother Pan made a cylindrical case to preserve it, with a lining of blue felt and covered with hand-stitched green leather.

Everything was as well organised as it could be. We had a letter of introduction from English Heritage to their official warden at Stonehenge. The order and timing of the rite had been worked out in detail together with the entry and exit processions and the places which we would occupy inside the circle of stones. Our officers were all experienced ritualists and the planetary invocations were memorised and polished through long practice and many occasions.

Stonehenge at first sight to me seemed small in contrast to the low rolling hills, and rather bleak and open to the cold overcast February sky. The ground was carpeted with snow, the near freezing temperatures perfect for the clarity of the ritual if uncomfortable for the celebrants. We parked our cars and found our caravan in the small carpark, which was connected to the site of the stones by a subway under the road, and we were welcomed by the English Heritage warden. Despite the unseasonable month there were a few cars and a coach in the carpark and a number of tourists wandering around.

We took three or four turns inside the confined space of the caravan to get our robes on. Then, when all of us were ready, we formed our procession and solemnly marched to the subway. In front was the Mars officer in a bright scarlet red robe, armed with a massive steel two-handed broadsword made by one of our members to the traditional design. Behind him came the Sun and Jupiter robed in rich purple and gold, carrying the wands of their office, then came the Mercury officer wearing orange and purple and carrying the Constitution rolled up in its case. The priestesses of the Moon and Venus followed, both wearing rich headdresses, the Moon robed in silver and bearing the thurible, Venus robed in emerald green and bearing the Cup. Then came the priestess of Saturn wearing black and carrying an hourglass; behind her came Uranus, Neptune, and finally Pluto, all walking in step and chanting in unison: "Holy art Thou, Lord of the Universe; Holy art Thou, Whom Nature hath not formed!"

In the subway we were met by a little crowd of Japanese tourists who flattened themselves against the walls, wide-eyed and speechless as we passed by. As we came up again, still chanting as we marched, we noticed a dozen or so people grouped in twos and threes around the perimeter fence, who pointed us out to each other but did not approach us. The snow crunched under our feet as we ended our chant and approached the entrance of the eastern trilithon. The stones were suddenly massive and looming in a ponderous greeting. The Mars officer made the sign of the Enterer and crossed the threshold, and we followed him into the circle of Stonehenge.

The Continuum of the O∴A∴A∴ at Stonehenge,
February 1986.

ALL THIS AND A BOOK

There was a great silent atmosphere inside the stones as of a magnificently old and almost benign Temple Spirit, enduring and very much alive and very protective of its integrity. The space inside was comfortably big enough for the ten of us although we were to one side of the centre because of the fallen stones lying there. We were very intimately surrounded with the ambient vitality of Stonehenge, and we opened the ceremony without delay.

The officer of Pluto made the statement of intent:

"Brothers and Sisters, we stand upon this ancient and most holy of places to celebrate the mysteries of the passage of time, and the conjunction of the Sun, the Moon, Mercury, Venus, and Jupiter, in the Mid-Heaven. It is our will to commemorate this moment with the inauguration of our Constitution, that by this harmonious combination of celestial influences we may attain the gifts and blessings of the Stars. So mote it be, Amen."

The Mercury officer then read aloud the Constitution. The Moon priestess gave the thurible to the Sun who blessed and ignited the charcoal and incense in the traditional manner and declared the temple open, whereupon Mercury performed the Lesser Banishing Rite of the Pentagram, and then took the thurible from the Sun and performed the Ritual of the Rose Cross, after which the thurible was returned to the Moon.

The rite had been carefully timed to ensure that each presiding officer could make his or her invocation and bless the Constitution and the talismans with the power and virtue of the planetary deity invoked as it passed overhead, and sign the Constitution at the moment of conjunction with the Mid-Heaven. This meant that there was a pause between the invocations of the Sun and of Venus, and then

Mercury and the Moon's invocations overlapped slightly; the time was measured by Saturn. During their invocations the voices of the officers became peculiarly resonant, as if the sound was harmonised with the frequencies of the stones themselves; the Moon's vocal timbre seemed to echo from the huge stone behind her. It was noted that the cloud cover directly above the stones parted to reveal a circle of clear blue sky above us.

Finally, the officers of Mars, Saturn, Uranus, Neptune and Pluto signed their names on the Constitution and the seals of our Order were attached as the Moon went conjunct Jupiter, the last aspect before She left the sign. The ceremony was closed by Pluto and we left the circle, led by the Sun, Jupiter, and Venus, and followed at the rear by Mars. The warden came out and opened the boundary ropes for us to pass through. We met another set of tourists in the subway, who parted before us in much the same way as the first lot had done.

Back in the caravan we were unusually quiet as the kettle went onto the stove. Tea was made. A cooked stew had been transported in two pressure cookers and was heated up. Robes were taken off and folded, magical weapons placed in safety. Bread was buttered. At last the feast was served up, and consumed to the last drop and crumb. We packed up our things and headed for home, still subdued, lost in our own impressions of the ritual in the stones. It had been unlike anything we had ever experienced before.

Our robes, richly made in the colours of the King Scale of the Kabbalah for this ritual, were never worn again, nor were any of the weapons ever used after Stonehenge. We had become completely magically depolarised and many members simply returned to normal life, having little memory of the work they had done, and so it was left to another part of The Continuum of the O.'.A.'.A.'. to properly close the circle. They did not turn back and look at what they had left behind, they just walked forward into the obscurity from whence they came, and never met again and never performed another magickal ritual; thus the integrity of the Rite was preserved and the Great Temple was once more sealed astrally and physically.

The wider purpose of the Stonehenge Ritual was to revivify the magick of old England using the harmonised planetary forces, at the only place that was capable of refocusing them. The dissolution of the old aeon was bringing a worldwide abandonment of systems as whole nations went into a state of socio-psychological flux, but the power invoked at Stonehenge would rise phoenix-like and eventually radiate forth to inform the world once more. We were a singular group of magickians belonging to the most powerful occult organisation in the country, trained for this work for between ten and twenty years, and we purified and consecrated Stonehenge to a ritual unique in the history of the world. It would never be possible to bring ten such astrologically perfect people together again to embody their planetary deity and mediate that planet's forces to revivify the centre of the earth and to refocus its power. In many ways the combined power of the group was the sacrifice that had to be made in order to open the channel so that celestial power would then again flow through.

We had taken some photographs of the purification ceremony in the Stonehenge circle, though the rite itself could not be photographed as it would have been profaned, and at the end of the 1980's they were all that remained. I seemed to be the last group member in town who was still magickally active; even the negatives had gone. Jim said, "Everything has a beginning, a middle, and an end. And that was the end of that group. There was simply no more for them to do." Trevor returned to the West Country where Jake was continuing his work with the English Qaballa, taking with him copies of his computer software, a quantity of ritual equipment, and a sheaf of Jim's notes. To make it easy for them to publish their research Jim also handed on *The New Equinox/British Journal of Magick* magazine format, and then he went into magickal retirement.

I had no other alternative life to slip into, and I did not want one either. My Quest was not finished, though my Dark Night was drawing to a close, but I still had questions unanswered, and so I was content to go on as I had been. I began the daily practice of Pranayama in the padmasana or Lotus position, meditating on the Kundalini centre, and after two or three years I achieved results that answered the descriptions in the books. I constructed short planetary rituals for myself, usually involving Fortuna and Venus, and slowly the boat of my Soul steadied and life assumed the appearance of orderliness once more. I was on my own, but I no longer minded; the night terrors had ceased and there were traces of a dawning light on the horizon of my desert darkness, and one bright star rising high in its firmament.

My painting became problematic as I sought for images and compositions to express what I saw and felt to be sacred and true; eventually, sitting in an art gallery under a Burne-Jones of exceptional emotional content, I wept as I realised that the pictures I wanted to make had already been made, and with more skill than I could ever possess. I went back to my roots and worked with watercolour for a time, producing some fairly decent landscape and animal studies, and I made some marquetry boxes and clock-faces as well, learning how to construct the Celtic knotwork designs used in the extraordinary miniatures in the *Book of Kells*.

But my Muse seemed to have packed her bags and gone on holiday; the only satisfactory creative expression seemed to be literary in nature, and I rather wanted to write a book about the English Qaballa. (I eventually did this in 2016.) I had already edited some of Jim's notes and composed one or two little essays on English Qaballa, and Jim was beginning to trust me with his writing to the extent of asking me to put articles together from his work, and do two versions, one with and one without the E. Qaballistic calculations. I was able to demonstrate that I understood his analyses and followed his proposed hypotheses through to synthesis with a wide range of systems and disciplines; at the same time, of course, it was all making the connections with my own psyche, for with reading and typing and editing his notes I was absorbing huge amounts of occult wisdom and my mind was constantly being stretched and reshaped.

I saw the deities of the old myths not as powerful superhumans accessible via a sort of Narnian filing cabinet, but as living and present forces with particular characteristics, inhabiting the material substance of their planets and constellations, infusing their Weapons and other things attributed to them, and symbolised by their E. Qaballistic values which connected their individualities unequivocally into my own evolving cosmological pattern.

I learned to think in opposites and abstracts. Everything was possible and nothing was real. The Universe was perfectly imperfect. The available evidence suggested a causal singularity but it was impossible to be sure except by personal gnosis, and as I was beginning to notice, one can know something without ever realising it or understanding it. But the whole of Creation was for love's sake and done by the power of love; I saw love and lust throughout nature and I exulted in it.

One afternoon Jim challenged me to see God in a matchbox. I accordingly went home and settled myself in front of a box of Swan Vestas. Eventually I found God in the matchbox by keeping still and quiet and feeling with my intuition and my love-under-will until the connection was made between the life in me and the life in it; it took three or four hours, I think, and taught me much about the magickal technique of concentration. Another exercise was adapted from Crowley's "Jugorum", in which I rapped my knuckles with the edge of a ruler or brought them down across the edge of a table instead of employing a razor and scarring myself; I continued this until the proper result was obtained.

I adapted one of Jim's methods of analysis to suit my preference for contemplation. As a contemplative exercise I would imagine myself waking in a prehistoric cave with no memories or preconceived ideas. I got up and went outside, and the first thing that I saw would be the subject I was interested in examining. I cast myself as the observer in the story, and allowed temporal plasticity so that I could collect and analyse data, and attempted to assess my reaction to natural phenomena, such as the Sun. When I first saw the big warm brightness and felt its life-giving radiance shining in the sky, I was seeing something that was above me and vastly greater, casting its light to the furthest extent of my vision. The heat was pleasant on the skin, but too much of it made a reddened soreness, and its brilliance left blinding after-images in my eyesight; this entity warranted respect. I could watch it vanishing in the west and rising again in the east, but I might skip the experiences of twilight and starlight and moonlight, concentrating instead on the solar power. I would observe the changes of the daily cycle, and the movement of shadows, and how the places of dawn and sunset moved back and forth across the horizon, and I would mark the solstices and the equinoxes to measure the year and predict the seasons. By keeping everything very simple and idealised and as new and unadulterated as I could, I gained insights into basic phenomena worn familiar with study and custom, and sharpened up their blunted edges.

I read Bardon's *Initiation Into Hermetics* and adapted some of the operations for my own purposes, and feeling the desire to stretch my magical muscles I turned to the Bornless Rite, which I copied out from Crowley's *Magick in Theory and Practice* into a new notebook of the "Book of Shadows" variety. I practised it every morning for a month, after which I felt I had learned enough to begin proper performance of the ritual for a given period; I went on with this morning exercise for a further four months, and it yielded the appropriate results.

I continued my studies of Astrology, and found an opportunity to put what I had learned to good use. The son of one of the group members had recently split up with his girlfriend; she had dumped him acrimoniously, and he wanted her back. He asked me if I could do anything, and after consulting the ephemeris I told him to ask me again in a few hours' time. He did so, and I made my invocations and drew the talisman accordingly. I could not promise a permanent reunion, I told him, but you'll have her back by the end of the week. Sure enough, the young lady in question appeared, properly contrite and regretful of losing such a desirable mate; however, his pride had been damaged along with his heart, and as soon as he was sure of her he gently let her go. They went their separate ways and remained good friends.

It was the late 1980's, after Stonehenge, and Jim's work with the English Qaballa had begun to focus again on the sequence of 28 characters in AL Ch. II v. 76. The solution has been described at length elsewhere; briefly, the sequence is split into two sets of ten characters which delineate the branches and the roots of a Complete Tree. The eight central characters L G M O R 3 Y X are seen as the trunk, having the value 93 (=DIVIDE, UNITY, NATURE, TIME, MOTHER). The first section, having the same value as LIBRA, 58, signifies the perfect balance of Heaven, and the last section is its manifestation as the ten numbers and letters add to 200, the value of MANIFESTATION. This composite symbol assigns the ten Sephiroth of the traditional Hebrew pattern to the roots of *Liber AL*'s Tree, whose Heavenly branches are arranged as the Perfected Tree with Malkuth in Daath.

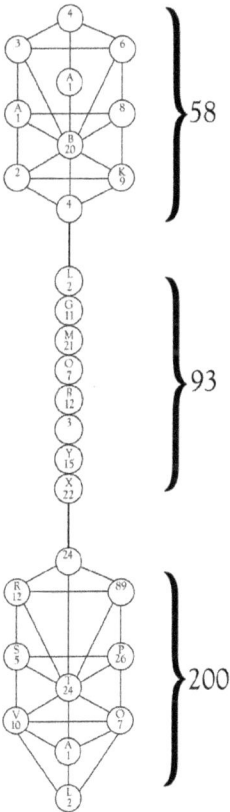

A variety of E. Qaballistic techniques had been developed for working with the Complete Tree, or "Two-seventy-six," as we referred to the collection of numbers and letters. The pattern of 28 spheres was both a key and a template which would unlock any chosen number, and since we wished to investigate the mysteries of TIME=93 and NATURE=93 and that which formed the trunk of our Tree, the DIVIDE=93 and UNITY=93 between the roots of Manifestation and the branches in Heaven, so that number was found the most useful.

Heaven, the Top Tree in E. Qaballistic terms, was an unmanifested state of perfect balance signified by $(4+6+3+8+A=1+B=20+K=9+2+4+A=1) = 58 =$ HOUSE and LIBRA and HADIT, described as the "secret centre", "everywhere the centre", to "be found...never", and "the complement of Nu". Particle physics confirmed Hadit as the infinitely tiny disturbance in space hidden by the visible wave-form of NU=31. Jim had shown me how the shapes of the letters and numbers concealed and revealed this secret: the combination of the horizontal wave of NU and the vertical wave-form of the letter S made the word SUN, whose light had been shown to have characteristics of both particles and wave-forms.

All of this (except the physics) had been explained in TNE/BJM Volume 6 Part 1, where Jim had also remarked that, "Kenneth Grant postulated the existence of two Trees of Life and it is a tribute to this magickian's ability that without the Qaballistic Key to *Liber AL* he produced results that parallel some of our own. However, there is a limit to how much accurate information can be gleaned from Astral Contact due to interference from the Lord of Dispersion (93) who gives results that are right for the wrong reasons and wrong for the right reasons. (See Grant's comments on the works of Lovecraft and A.O. Spare in his *Typhonian Trilogy* for illustrations of this phenomenon.)

"Only pure numbers reveal the truth and it is against pure numbers that astral visions must be checked for their validity. It is against the background of pure numbers that the Class A material must be examined, for without the role of number "these runes" become extremely dangerous, leading one into the minefield of 93. Pure number has always been the way of the magickian; apart from a few diversions into hallucinated art and literature, anything else is always at best mysticism and at worst insanity...

"The Complete Tree of Life that is II:76 is the answer to the problem posed in AL I:45-7: 'The Perfect and the Perfect are one Perfect and not two; nay, are none! Nothing is a secret key of this law. Sixty-one the Jews call it; I call it eight, eighty, four hundred & eighteen. But they have the half: unite by thine art so that all disappear.' 8, 80 and 418 correspond with the three forms of Nothing delineated by the Hebrew Kabbalah as the levels of existence beyond Kether, but this alone is an unsatisfactory description of Life Eternal. The study of the Hebrew Tree will only give half the story of creation. In the Hebrew system nothing exists beyond Kether except the inexpressible veils of Negative existence. In the Complete Tree system the veils of Negative existence give way to a Perfect Tree of Life. Meditation on this Complete Tree makes all the systems of the psyche work in integrated harmony. This is because there is no negative existence and there is a place for all the energy of the spirit to go, thus permitting no leakage of force into spurious negative existence where it can be allowed to breed monsters of Gods who need no justification for their actions. All powers on the Complete Tree justify their actions by being part of the cycle of life, the complete cycle of life. The Tree indicated by II:76 is truly the blueprint upon which any system in human experience can be explained in terms of natural phenomena."

The Hebrew Tree as I understood it described the visible and manifest microcosm which could be experienced by and in my human consciousness, as the roots of the Complete Tree whose branches were in Heaven. I had imprinted the living pattern of II:76 on my mind in my E.Qaballistic studies and daily meditations, where it shaped my understanding of Creation and the division for love's sake. The repetition of the letter "A" in the Manifest Yesod, the mind-mirror of consciousness, and twice in Heaven in the perfected Malkuth-Daath and in Geburah, gave me a credible account of how one might ascend to that promised bliss, and a reason why one did not encounter the souls of the dead while in meditation upon the Middle Pillar; reading from top to bottom the repeated symbol gave a sequence which was the story of the Fall.

At Jim's suggestion I had drawn up the diagram of the two Trees and made copies with the E.Q. attributions filled in, and some with the spheres left blank to facilitate the study of particular numbers. Now I made half a dozen copies on A1 paper for Jim to annotate and work with as he investigated *Liber AL*'s delineation of the three forms of Nothing described by the Hebrew Kabbalists. We had a number of intense discussions about the various forms of Nothing, Zero, Nought, Negativity, and non-existence; I would go home with a blur where my mind had been.

One evening about eighteen months after the Stonehenge Rite, Jim showed me the pages of notes he had been making as he investigated the composite symbol, working at the mysteries still contained in the numbers and the words. The addition of 93 to the values of the twenty-eight characters made the spheres of Kether and Yesod in Heaven add up to 97, the value of NOTHING, a good word, for it is the reward of HEAVEN = 79, and descriptive of that existence beyond the dimensions of time and space. Also, 97 = PISCES, indicating the stage of the Zodiacal life-cycle preceding birth in ARIES = 66 = EARTH and BABE.

I was following Jim's introduction closely, and so he went on. 97 is the value of RA HOOR KHUT, he reminded me, and this was where his recent researches had started, with the first words of *Liber AL* III, "Abrahadabra! the reward of Ra Hoor Khut."

He had split the 11-letter word into three parts, ABRA = 34, HAD = 11, ABRA = 34, and looking at the numbers he saw 34 = TWO. He wrote 2, 11, 2 and regrouped the numbers to read 21, 12. These numbers were the values of M and R, two letters at the centre of the 93 section of II:76 with the negativity of the Goddess expressed as ∩ = 7 between them. Written together they make the symbol of Virgo and as 21,O,12 they made a very interesting glyph. Jim gave me several pages of notes to be typed and printed, for there were many threads weaving this bit of the story together. Reading, typing, and understanding this material all at once was an incredible experience, expanding the realms of my consciousness as if my mind were dough that had been leavened.

The following is an excerpt from Jim's notes of this period, as tidied up by me at the time.

"An examination of the word ABRAHADABRA = 79 was essential in testing the symbolism of the Two Trees since its reward, 97, is the value of Kether and Yesod on the Perfect Tree. The first verse of AL's third Chapter states "Abrahadabra; the reward of Ra Hoor Khut." RA HOOR KHUT = 97 = NOTHING and its reward is ABRAHADABRA = 79 = HEAVEN; the reversal of the number gives its reward. The word has eleven letters which are in three parts, ABRA = 34, HAD = 11, and ABRA = 34. 34 is the value of LEO, so that the Word may be sigilised as ♌11♌; TWO also has the value 34, making the sigil 2112, a sequence of numbers that appears at the centre of II:76 where the letters M,O,R, have the values 21,7,12. 7 is the value of O and is thus interchangeable with Zero so that our sigil becomes 21012. These numbers rehearse the progression from Zero or Nothing, to one, and two. In the centre of the 93 section, Nothing or Zero is divided and creation takes place. Thus we find that Abrahadabra is the sigil of creation – naturally, if it is the ENDING = 93 of the words (see AL III:75, "The ending of the words is the Word Abrahadabra") it must also be the beginning, and BEGIN = 93.

"HAD = 11, "the manifestation of Nuit," (AL I:1) is at the centre of the Word. The number 11 is 1 and 1 or one and one where ONE = 46 = WOMAN: the Great Goddess Nuit's manifestation is therefore a division into two goddesses. The concepts of the Goddess Nuit are an emphatic Zero: NUIT has the value 78 where 7 = O or Zero, and 8 or ∞ is infinity, meaning that Nuit is Nothing to Infinity. 97 = NOTHING and PISCES, indicating via the symbolism of the Fish that the essential nature of the ideas resonated by the numbers 97 and 79 is that of female sexuality. 7 is the number of the Goddess and 9 the number of Yesod which rules the sex organs. We may conclude that

Abrahadabra and Ra Hoor Khut refer to the divine sexuality that unites and divides the Goddess, or more correctly they are the names of the generative organs of the Goddess as seen on two different planes. This is borne out by the fact that the word Abrahadabra begins and ends the third chapter and is referred to as a secret key. This conclusion is further confirmed by the word REWARD=59, the value of YONI, a word found elsewhere in the class A material. Accordingly, the Sigil of the Word is refined to)II(to incorporate the shape of the symbol of Pisces, ♓.

The Word that was the "ending of the Words" had revealed itself as a Word of Creation and Birth, enshrined in the heart of 93=VIRGIN, MOTHER, and TIME. It was a demonstration of how Unmanifest divine power came into the realm of the primal manifest archetype. "None, and two," breathed the faery light of the Star Goddess, and there she was in that round letter "O" and the ELEVEN that had the same value as DIVISION, 101 and was the number of HAD=11.

My mind fizzed and bloomed and gently exploded as the symmetry of the division for love's sake became apparent throughout the 93 section, showering down into manifest Kether and descending to a balanced duality in Malkuth. 34=LEO, which Jim had written sideways to make a glyph similar to the symbol of Pisces, which itself resembled the shape of the letter "H". With the value 4, H was the initial letter of the first word of *Liber AL*, and the first character of II:76.

Our agreed shorthand for ABRAHADABRA became)II(or (II), and we would not speak the Word aloud but referred to "the eleven-letter Word". This was a rich vein that Jim had struck which yielded an enormous quantity of notes, nearly doubling my archive; I drew up the graphic presentation of the glyph's evolution.

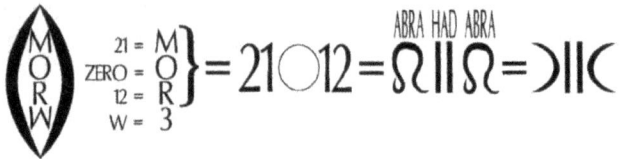

Our Creation Story was demonstrably complete, and we had at least three forms of Nothing in our philosophy. We began with the Supreme Negativity of Nothing-before-there-was-anything – which for convenience we thought of as hermaphroditic/female, though we knew that the whole concept was so far removed from logical thought and symbolic attributions that it was merely for the sake of our intellect that we made such correspondences – this unimaginable Zero state divided itself into Nothing and less-than-Nothing for it could not by division become more than itself. By multiplication these two Negatives (or goddesses) combined to make a positive force in accordance with mathematical principles, which to all intents and purposes was a God, a positive particle symbolised by the equal-armed cross, +.

The Creation of the Manifest Universe can only be described in poetic terms for it transcends word, thought and image, and Time and Space: *Liber AL* presents us with a Creation Story beginning with Nothing dividing itself into two negatives which then combine to produce a positive. "...I am none and two. I am divided for love's sake, for the chance of union. This is the creation of the world." (I have condensed *Liber AL* I:28-30 slightly for clarity.)

All the negatives in the Creation story in the *Book of the Law* signify the feminine, as a woman's polarity is negative to the world (and a man's is positive). The double negative is symbolised by two Goddesses united by Love. It is the difference between them which is positive that divides them again.

The motif of two observably alike phenomena divided and united by a third is repeated many times in the natural world; for example, the roots and branches of a tree which have a similar form are separated by the trunk which is quite a different structure. The story is expressed in the mathematical rule where two negative or minus numbers always multiply to a positive number, which is a basic factual truth, an undeniable parallel with the system revealed in *Liber AL* which thereby demonstrates its validity. The structure of the symbol is actually rather common once one learns to recognise it: the *fleur de lys*, the caduceus, the winged disk, all rehearse the same pattern. The composite symbol that is the Complete Tree of Life of AL II:76, also known as the Two Trees, has the same shape, of two that are alike, separated and united by one that is different.

The Perfect Tree manifests from O in LGMOR3YX; these eight characters have the value 93 which is the value of UNITY and DIVIDE and MOTHER, so it is clear that the 93 section of II:76 has within it the apparatus of Creation. Indeed, at the centre we find M=21 and R=12 on either side of O, which together reveal the sequence 21-O-12, illustrating the progression of Creation. The O has the value 7 which is the number of the Goddess; thus it is a symbol of negativity, and can be seen in this context as the Yoni of the Goddess. There are 3 characters on one side and 4 on the other. If there were 3 or 4 characters on both sides of Nothing then manifestation could not occur, because Nothing would be balanced. (See the Judgement Hall of Osiris for details). With the number 97=NOTHING appearing twice on the Perfect Tree as well, in Kether and Yesod, we have the three forms of Nothing indicated by AL I:46 "...eight, eighty, four hundred & eighteen."

Above (or preceding) MOR we find the letter G. This letter has the same value as HAD=11=G. In the manuscript of II:76 the letter G is written with two crossbars instead of the usual one: it is the first symbol upwards from the Abrahadabra-Ra Hoor Khut complex, and the shape represents the entrance into Nothing, the pathway between being and non-being. One may conclude that Had is expelled upwards from the sex organs of Nuit. The letter which follows is L=2. This duality is already prefaced in the number eleven.

Below the 2112 formula we find the unmanifest of the Lower Tree, consisting of 3=W, Y=15, X=22, which are the equivalents of the Hebrew Ain Soph Aur, Ain Soph, and Ain. The three nothings indicated by the number 3 have become three somethings, three interferences in non-existence have produced in their turn three dimensions or directions (Y), which generate a fourth expressed in the cross (X) which as all Kabballists know is resumed as a symbol on every sphere of the Middle Pillar. The numerical value of X is 22, the number of paths on the manifest Tree of Life.

I must point out that the number 93 is used to reveal the correspondences of the Upper and Lower Trees. 93 is the value of NATURE and TIME and therefore by addition it unlocks the values of the Sephiroth in Heaven and in Manifestation and reveals the manner in which they become comprehensible to us in the matrix of Time and Nature.

117 is the value of Kether on the Tree of manifestation where 1=ONE=WOMAN and 7 is the number of Venus the Goddess of Love. This means that manifestation begins with the Goddess, divided for love's sake into two Women (1 and 1) and a Goddess (7). 117 is the value of GEMINI, Ⅱ, which is the sign of the Zodiac attributed to the Tarot Trump the Lovers. It is worth noting that in his Thoth Tarot Crowley places two female figures at the top of the card, and in his *Book of Thoth* states that "in its original form, it was the story of Creation". The card is also known as the Brothers which is why the women of the A.'. A.'. are said to be the Brothers of that Order.

This apparent duality is repeatedly resumed in the system of the Two Trees. The creation partakes of the nature of its creator. The unmanifest Kether has the number 97 which is the value of Pisces, ♓, another 'double' Zodiacal sign. As we have shown, the word Abrahadabra resumes the characters at the centre of the 93 section in the numbers 2112.)II(recalls the shapes of Pisces and Gemini; LEO=34=TWO and SHE: the word of the source of creation is again emphatically representative of two females.

These two Women of Gemini are pure negative concepts. The influence from on high causes them to change in accordance with the Will of the unmanifest. The traditional lightning flash of the Hebrew system cannot work as there is no real interplay of forces on the Tree. The true course of manifestation takes two directions at once. This is the real reason why the diagonal across the Tree is the upper power on a lower arc. Where the two Women meet they form a cross, creating a male power: – x – = +. Two negatives make a positive. The most basic phenomena of maths and physics confirms the supremacy of the female archetype. Woman, because of her negative polarity, is capable of creation, as well as reproduction.

The Goddess alone, the primal negativity, divided herself into two negatives, which then combined again to produce a positive particle, a God. The purpose and function of this God-child is to perform His Mother's will; he is after all the positive manifestation of the Will of the Goddess. In action the positive particle becomes unstable, implementing changes in accordance with its destiny which is ultimately to return to the Zero state. The positive particle is symbolised by the equal-armed cross, and the unstable positive particle is symbolised by the Calvary cross.

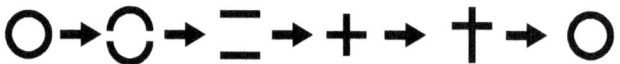

$$O \rightarrow \bigcirc \rightarrow = \rightarrow + \rightarrow \dagger \rightarrow O$$

The positive particle is Hadit, the infinitely small disturbance in space, the slight imperfection without which the Universe would cease to exist. The process by which change occurs is symbolised by 93, which ensures that the unexpected will always happen, that the impossible will become necessary. The old concept of only one Tree of Life is untenable because nothing could happen in manifestation beyond the production of the amoeba – a single celled creature. This is obvious, as a system going from zero to manifestation could only produce this without periodic interference from beyond, i.e., from 93.

Liber AL speaks of the Creation in the present tense because it is continuously happening. It is not an event that happened at some point in the dim and distant past. The Creation partakes of the nature of the Creator, and

GOD=24=NOW. TIME=93 is COILING=93 through Eternity causing CHANGE=68=LIFE to occur. Concepts of the Creation are unacceptable to the rational mind because the Creation happens on all levels of being, most of which are much more sophisticated than Reason. The modern scientific view is equally illogical and reflects the twentieth century's enthusiasm for bigger and bigger explosions. As a man is, so he sees: the E. Qaballist sees a coherent Universe in which Nature does not create with forceful explosions but by subtle stages of unpredictable development. We were pleased to find that THE BIG BANG = 153 = CONSCIOUSNESS, aligning our ideas with the metaphysical side of particle physics.

All sorts of correspondences suggested themselves and a variety of stories and symbols unlocked their secrets with the application of the Creation Formula. We began to understand the mechanism by which a magickal spell actually works, and how the mystery of 93 is woven into all.

CREPUSCULAR WAYPOINT CONFIGURATION

THE INTERNET WAS just starting to bud at the end of the 1980's, and although the dial-up modem connection was slow and unreliable, there was a discernible occult community online. Jake had a busy site and was spreading the English Qaballistic word wherever it would go. He and Trevor were publishing issues of *The Equinox/British Journal of Thelema*; they had been working extensively with astrologically synchronised ritual and in particular with the Part of Fortune, and expanding the English Qaballa into techniques of spirit evocation. Their work was done in isolation and there had been little communication since the Stonehenge period. Jim wanted to be left alone, which suited everyone concerned but inevitably led to a divergence of approach which I found regrettable but had no power to resolve.

Then came Allen Greenfield's book *Secret Ciphers of the Ufonauts* which irritated me with its inaccuracies; Jim did not care. He had a much wider lens on the scene than I, and was initially unimpressed by the internet, so it was I who opened Greenfield's email when he wrote asking if Jim was the discoverer of the English Qaballa, and then typed Jim's laconic reply, "Yup!" We found the ideas of alien contact interesting, but the errors were not corrected and we heard no more from Mr Greenfield.

We had been observing the effect of Pluto as he made his way through Scorpio and into Sagittarius. The two Signs are part of the English Qaballistic Quaternary Formula, LIBRA + SCORPIO + SAGITTARIUS + CAPRICORN

(58+93+146+121) = 418, which we had been studying for over a decade. Briefly, the four stages are judgement, death, refinement, and transformation; since Pluto governs the multitudes his effect is to make history happen, and is best seen with hindsight. However, the early analyses of the 418 cycle were being proved as the world we had known died in the 1980's and global communication became the order of the day. The century was drawing to a close as Pluto traversed the Sign of Religion and Philosophy, and made both metaphorical and physical long distance travel into fashionable pastimes. The global village was becoming a reality, humanity was waking up to the diversity of its apprehension of the Divine, and in our own country legislation about religious tolerance brought all kinds of customs and ceremonies into the public view.

Occultism began to find a renaissance coming on. It appeared that a large number of people were expecting a New Age or were of the opinion that it had already arrived, and there was a collective sense of a new light on the horizon at the dawn of the twenty-first century. Our studies tended to confirm this, and we anticipated that Pluto in Capricorn would signify a transformation in consciousness.

I started to feel an urgent need to establish Jim's name and reputation amongst occultists in Europe and America. I also had a long-standing ambition to produce a properly bound and fully enumerated *Book of the Law*; I had tried and failed to re-invent the technique called "perfect binding" wherein the single pages are held as a solid block and strings are glued into notches cut in the back edge, and realising that I needed the right equipment I vowed to purchase the necessary tools and materials and teach myself bookbinding, and make a hardback edition of

Liber AL – when the money arrived. In 1993 I inherited a sufficient sum to undertake the project. I remembered how once as a child I had dropped a cheap paperback; the glue had gone and the loose pages fanned out in a catastrophic flow, spreading sheets of paper all over the floor. As I gathered them up and innocently tried to reassemble the book my late father said wryly, "I see you're going to be a bookbinder one day!"

I achieved moderate success with my privately published and limited edition of *Liber AL*. I used the Kaaba imprint and acquired a set of ISBN's, and I wrote and printed two copies of an early handbook of English Qaballa to practise book-binding. Each copy of *Liber AL*, published in 1995 under the title "L" was a triumph for me. I went to great lengths to produce the Comment according to instructions, "...in red ink and black upon beautiful paper made by hand..." and each book was numbered and contained its own uniquely coloured illustrations of the two unicursal 26-pointed stars. The binding style was the strongest and most enduring method that I could find, and I did my best, but the volumes would not have won any prizes for craftsmanship.

I made a small website to advertise the book, and sold a number of copies. I was pleased because I had composed an introduction identifying James Lees as the discoverer of the English Qaballa, and giving the correct date, November 1976, and I felt that it was important to get this information published and in the public domain. There was already dissension brewing over the name that Jim had chosen for the system, and a swarm of alternative spellings and acronyms, and I worried needlessly for a while about the effects of disinformation. It was obvious upon reflection however that the forces responsible for the Qaballa and the *Book* could very well look after it, come what may.

It seemed a good idea for us to join in though, and so I became a website manager and designer and published the archive online in its entirety. We kept the structure of my cross-indexing with multiple pages of contents lists linked to more pages of text. The site was not easy to navigate or to read with its screenfuls of blank prose, and as we explored the internet ourselves we redesigned the site several times. We removed some material, and from time to time we added new remarks, including some accurate predictions based on aspects to Pluto in the first decade of the century. Some time in that period I attained a second verifiable Vision in which all my sorrows turned to the purest joy as I was shown how we live forever and what a joyously ecstatic miracle it is that the Universe should be thus.

English Qaballa seemed to have stalled at the end of the century. Jake's campaign was coming to an end, and we detected traces of disagreement in certain quarters, and a distinct tone of frustration and hostility. In America the QBLH were extending their own researches with a Qaballistic evaluation computer program called Lexicon, written by Tina Coutu, and Joel Love's experiments with alternative alphabet codes, assisted by Tom Chaudoin, who continued the work after Joel's untimely death.

Elsewhere Jim's discovery had been picked up and toyed with, re-named and regurgitated in unrecognisable forms, and it was nicely obscured in an article compiled (and frequently altered, edited, and re-edited) in Wikipedia, the online encyclopaedia. Greenfield's errors were repeated, and suddenly there was a variety of alpha-numeric systems based on the English Alphabet. After I became a published writer in 2016 I was in a position to correct the Wikipedia article once and for all, and cheerfully did so.

For a while we were interested by the burgeoning conspiracy-theory community which was researching and publishing all sorts of Rosicrucian and Freemasonic traditions, and details of sacred geometry and astrophysics and geophysical archaeology. It was a lot of information that we would have found difficult to compile ourselves, which served to enhance our already integrated and organically harmonised English Qaballistic world view. We were way ahead of them all.

There was a problem still unsolved in the English Qaballistic interpretation of *Liber AL* which revolved around the expression "I am." This simple statement is really very difficult, for what archetypal entity can say "I am"? The Goddesses are all negative and their utterances are a different mystery altogether; the Gods all say "I will be", since they are in a continuous state of becoming and therefore cannot stop to identify with a particular quality and say "I am this". Yet *Liber AL* has many occurrences of this phrase, one of the most interesting being in Chapter II verse 6, "I am Life, and the giver of Life".

This could not be Horus speaking, despite the numbers adding up, for the characteristics of Horus do not incline towards life and the giving of life. He is an Avenging God and his function is to slay rather than to create, but the words "I AM" have the same value as HORUS, 45, and this number is unhelpfully the value of NOT and BE as well. A further difficulty with AL II:6 "I am Life", was that LIFE=JESUS, and AL III has some very odd things to say about the relationship between the Hawk-Headed God and the Crucified God.

It was a conundrum that we had often puzzled over without reaching a satisfactory conclusion.

One day in 2006 or 2007 Jim and I were sitting in the kitchen talking E.Q. and once again going over the problem of I AM. On what seemed a whim I took pen and paper and did the "counting well" calculation with the two words. What I came up with shook me to my core.

"You're not going to believe this," I said, looking up, and trembling as I spoke.

"What?" Jim said disinterestedly.

"I've just done I AM counted well, and, um..."

"Yes?"

"And it comes to sixty-eight."

My words seemed to echo in the sudden utter stillness, and reverberate out into the silent Universe.

"Are you sure?"

Wordlessly I gave him my piece of paper. His eyes were wide and shining as he looked at it and then at me. "You clever little lady," he said at last.

There was a new quality to the light in the room, clearer, brighter, more golden, and just on the edge of audibility I seemed to hear angelic choirs uplifted in a paean of joy. Nothing would ever be quite the same as before the birth-moment of this idea, when the quintessence of HORUS/I AM was revealed in JESUS/LIFE. The God of Life can say I AM because I AM at its very soul is LIFE. The Biblical Jesus promises eternal life, but only Life can produce Life. Thus the meaning of "I am Life and the giver of Life" became clear, and when we remembered that "I AM LIFE" adds up to 113 which is the value of Tiphareth on the Top Tree of II:76, we knew we were on the right track. (The letter "B" (=20) is ascribed to the Heavenly

Tiphareth in AL II:76, and by adding 93 we can begin to understand how the Sephirah exists in TIME=93 + 20 =113 = I AM LIFE/JESUS). The Jesus of the *Book of the Law* was the King of Heaven, and there was no doubt of it.

There is no letter J in Hebrew, and the English spelling of Jesus did not appear until the translation of the Gospels, which means that Jesus as He is shown to the E. Qaballist is not the same character as the God of the Christians. He is more like the Good Shepherd that we were taught about as children. His number, 68, means Infinite Law in E.Q., as has been explained at length in an earlier work. He is the Life in everything, you, me, and the Universe, and all the angels and spirits and demons and gods and devils, and all the birds and trees and insects, and the rocks and stones, and all the space in between things, and the very air we breathe. All our spells and invocations can be done in the Name of the Lord whose number is 68, for why appeal to the workers when we can approach the boss? The King of Heaven has dominion over all, and that is why prayers to Him are always answered, even if the answer is not the one that the faithful heart would have wished and hoped for.

We talked and talked for days, and Jim wrote pages of notes which I typed up on the laptop. An enormous area had been opened for our E. Qaballistic explorations. It is a mystery to me why nobody had done the counting well of I AM before; the only conclusion is that the time was not right for that seed to germinate, and our hearts and minds were unprepared for the glory that spread from the moment that it did come into being.

One of the first questions to arise was "How did Life come about in the first place?" The answer was right in front of us. Jesus was a Virgin birth as all Gods are, and both VIRGIN and MOTHER have the value 93 by English Qaballa. 93 is also the value of TIME. Time gives birth to Life – but there is a third part to this equation. The Holy Ghost, or the Will of God, or more simply God Himself, must be represented. So we looked for Him, and found that GOD=24=NOW.

Suddenly we had a Trinity, a proper functional Triad of powers that supported each other and depended on each other – Now, Life, and Time, also known as God, the Son of God, and the Virgin Mother – three fundamental principles which are eternal, and infinite, and which stand above all others. Now is the focus of Life in Time; Life is the expression of Now in Time; Time is the matrix in which Life apprehends the Now.

Our studies of particle physics had taught us that phenomena exist in a latent state containing all possible variations at once, until an observation occurs, which collapses the probability wave and brings a result into manifestation. Schrodinger's cat is both alive and dead in the box, until the box is opened and somebody takes a reading of old Felix's life signs. The tree is permanently falling and not falling in the forest, the sound it may make is for the observer to hear. Atoms at absolute zero or as near as science is capable of attaining, exist in a fluidic incoherent mess, until they are observed, when they immediately pull themselves together and start to behave properly. From this we may deduce that at the Creation there must have been Life to observe the moment in Time which was the first Now. We remember that THE BIG BANG has the same value as CONSCIOUSNESS, 153. Our Trinity could not be denied by science, and no man of any faith or with none could argue with its simple logic. Time gives birth to Life in the Now. Life observes Now in Time. Now is experienced by Life in Time.

Returning to our Complete Tree system we found more wonderment, for the Winter Solstice when the Sun turned North and the light began to return as the days grew longer occurred on 21/12, meaning that the numeric glyph of the Elevenfold Word of Creation, the Reward of Nothing, was resumed in the date of the Solstice. It preceded the festival of the Birth of JESUS/LIFE by four days, the period being the three degrees allowed by astrology for a celestial body to come to its strength in a Sign. And the Sign that the Sun entered was Capricorn, the Goat with the Light between his Horns, the last Sign of the 418 cycle.

We saw that the entrance of Pluto into Capricorn was an ideal opportunity to test this hypothesis. We were in contact with a handful of O∴A∴A∴ members who were interested in the possibility of ritualising the event, and we did so on 21/12/08 with the Sun conjunct Pluto at 0 degrees Capricorn, at the same time inaugurating the O∴A∴A∴ Second Order. A short while later it was reported that Pluto had revealed a red hue to the astronomers who were watching him.

Following this we looked again at the 418 cycle with a view to ritualising the entire sequence. We proceeded very carefully with a series of meditations synchronised with the Moon's passage through the four Signs. When we were satisfied that we were on the right track and that our work was acceptable to the Company of Heaven, Jim wrote a set of rituals, and we observed the times and carefully performed the ceremony for each Sign of 418 as the Moon moved through them. Our meditations had prepared us to a certain extent for this work, but it was challenging and disturbing nonetheless.

We each appointed ourselves our own judge, jury, and executioner. We made confession, and when the Moon passed into Scorpio the sentence was carried out. The judgement was always the same, but the story continued, and we travelled in dark wildernesses, towards transformation in the returning of the Divine Light when the Moon reached Capricorn. The initiatory formula is somewhat similar to that of Crowley's "Pyramidos" but being synchronised with the lunar cycle it has additional effects including the harmonising of the operator with cosmic factors which are continually being renewed.

The cycle of Lunar 418 rituals was extremely potent, and when Jim was satisfied with them he wrote the Rituals for marking the Sun's passage through 418 from the Autumn Equinox to Midwinter. Those of us who undertook the first performance of this cycle did so as a Solar Pilgrimage, such a significant journey it seemed in that early September of 2010, and to those who succeeded and endured to the end there were given Crusader-style longswords engraved with the seals of our Order and their Magickal Name. In the course of the Pilgrimage we each constructed a Pantacle with the Symbol of the Work at the centre, symbolising the Way we had chosen, which was completed during the fourth and final Ritual.

On our website we posted an invitation to anyone who wanted to take part in this experiment, and so we were accompanied on our Pilgrimage by our old friend the Flaming Viking, and by QBLH member Joel Love, both of whom reached the Winter Solstice and received their Swords.

ALL THIS AND A BOOK

We had two or three new members who were interested in our past history as reported in the press a quarter of a century earlier. The day before the Autumn Equinox we took them to the woods to look for the old Circle. We found the general area, and Jim told us how he had buried a large copper panel engraved with an Enochian conjuration deep in the centre of the Circle; oddly enough, the Tablet was unearthed by local treasure hunters in December, and other artefacts were discovered within a year of our visit, but the whole wood seemed to have moved, the trees were not in the same positions and the rounded glade under the birch and beech trees was no longer visible.

We were marking the Equinox and beginning our first Solar Pilgrimage. We lit a small fire where we thought the Circle had been, a homage to the past and a sacrifice for our future and sat quietly for a while in the woodsmoke perfumed stillness.

My mind went back to that first balefire on that chilly November night, and the Initiating Officers in their coloured robes who had stopped me and questioned me as I was led forward by my Summoner. How weary I had become, blindfolded and bound, with my nerves wound up to screaming pitch in the darkness, stumbling along, not knowing: not knowing! – until at last I stood still while the cords at wrist and ankle were undone, and the tension of anticipation went tumbling insanely over the edge with a swoop of intense joyous fear. Somewhere near here I had knelt with my naked back in the warm glow of the balefire, and felt hands at the back of my head fumbling briefly at the fastening of the blindfold. Then the wrap of cloth is gone and I open my eyes and I see the steel point of a sword, bright and sharp and deadly and pointing down towards my throat, between neck and collarbone. My gaze follows the unwavering blade up to the steady hands and behind them the dark amber eyes that had waited for mine to look up. Eyes whose depths were strangely familiar, with an expression of amused curiosity, as if he were calculating the exact pressure needed to drive the death-blow cleanly home.

I heard a deep voice over my shoulder demanding,

"Are you now ready to take the Oath?"

My eyes did not blink from that quizzical stare as I answered firmly.

"Yes, I am ready."

...Outro

THE MEMBERS OF the O∴A∴A∴ Second Order continue with the research into *Liber AL* and the English Qaballa, and with the practice of Stellar Magick. In particular we have practised the Rites of the Lunar and Solar 418 Cycles continuously since they were written by Brother Leo in 2009. The noticeable effects agreed by the ritualists (whether new to the game or having years of experience) include a quality of Initiation smooth and true, even unto the Knowledge and Conversation of the Holy Guardian Angel, and an astro-magickal cosmological integration both holistic and organic, contained in the medium of Time, with a steady realignment of individual consciousness to the continuity of existence from life to life, yea, to the certainty of Life Eternal!

And fearless!